50 SECRETS
Nobody Tells You
in HOLLYWOOD

The Working Actor's Guide to
Avoiding Pitfalls and Supercharging Your Career

50 SECRETS Nobody Tells You in HOLLYWOOD

The Working Actor's Guide to
Avoiding Pitfalls and Supercharging Your Career

Mike Kimmel
Foreword by GiGi Erneta

Copyright © 2025 Mike Kimmel

All rights reserved.
No portion of this book may be reproduced or transmitted in any form or by any means, electronic or mechanical, including photocopying, recording, or by any information storage or retrieval system, except for the inclusion of brief quotations in reviews.

ISBN 978-1-953057-18-1 (paperback)
ISBN 978-1-953057-17-4 (hardback)
ISBN 978-1-953057-16-7 (ebook)

Library of Congress Control Number: 2025913367

50 Secrets Nobody Tells You in Hollywood:
The Working Actor's Guide to Avoiding Pitfalls and Supercharging Your Career
The Professional Actor Series: Book 5

Ben Rose Creative Arts
New York - Los Angeles

Publisher's Cataloging-in-Publication Data
provided by Five Rainbows Cataloging Services

Names: Kimmel, Mike, author. | Erneta, GiGi, writer of foreword.
Title: 50 secrets nobody tells you in Hollywood : the working actor's guide to avoiding pitfalls and super-charging your career / Mike Kimmel ; foreword by GiGi Erneta.
Description: Los Angeles : Ben Rose Creative Arts, 2025. | Series: Professional actor, bk. 5.
Identifiers: LCCN 2025913367 (print) | ISBN 978-1-953057-18-1 (paperback) | ISBN 978-1-953057-17-4 (hardcover) | ISBN 978-1-953057-16-7 (ebook)
Subjects: LCSH: Acting--Vocational guidance. | Performing arts--Vocational guidance. | Acting--Handbooks, manuals, etc. | Theater--Production and direction--Vocational guidance. | Monologues. | BISAC: PERFORMING ARTS / Acting & Auditioning. | PERFORMING ARTS / Business Aspects. | EDUCATION / Arts in Education.
Classification: LCC PN2055 .K56 2025 (print) | LCC PN2055 (ebook) | DDC 792.028--dc23.
Interior design by Booknook.biz

Praise for
50 Secrets Nobody Tells You in Hollywood

"Where was this book when I struggled in Hollywood in the mid 1980s? Mike has created the perfect guidebook to navigate the many boulevards in Hollywood!"

>CHUCK DISNEY
>Feature Film Producer
>Arizona Film Resource Coordinator

"I'm a big believer in learning from those who've achieved what you want to achieve. Mike Kimmel pulls together mentors from throughout our industry and explores their wisdom while adding his own."

>LAURA CAYOUETTE
>Actor-Author-Filmmaker
>*Django Unchained, The Dirty South, Treme, Queen Sugar, House of Cards, Like Son, Cut Off, Hate Crime, Convergence*

"What truly elevates this book is its sense of generosity; Kimmel never holds back knowledge, and every page feels like a conversation with a trusted mentor who has your best interests at heart. His guidance resonates far beyond acting; the lessons on perseverance, humility, and self-belief apply to anyone pursuing a creative dream."

>LOS ANGELES BOOK REVIEW

"Kudos to my good friend and forever mentor, Mike Kimmel, for creating this inspiring guidebook for all actors. This serves not only those breaking into the moving image industry. These "Secrets" are powerful reminders for all of us that common sense, integrity, humility … and simple, good manners truly matter. Use your brain and your heart to achieve success … and happiness!"

    SHARON GARRISON
    Actor-Producer
    Portrayed Judge Amelia Sanders on Drop Dead Diva,
    Salem, Game of Silence, Claws, Preacher, Midnight Special

"*50 Secrets* weaves together motivational quotes and invaluable insider knowledge to provide essential guidance for individuals embarking on the brave and exciting realm of artistic expression. Mike Kimmel takes on the role of mentor, steering readers through the challenges of the industry, offering wisdom on navigating red flags, highlighting best practices, and emphasizing the importance of self-care. Consider *50 Secrets* your personal empowerment tool, which filters out the noise, allowing you to remain resolutely focused on your most meaningful goals."

    TRACEY L. ADLAI
    Founder-Director, The Valley Film Festival

"Any aspiring actor who wants to avoid heartbreak on the long and winding path to success should read this book immediately. Long-time actor Mike Kimmel reveals his hard-won insights from within the entertainment world, so new actors of all kinds can sidestep Hollywood's pitfalls. If you're currently wading into the film industry, this is a must-read!"

>Nora Isabel Cross
>Actor-Director-Producer, SheFilms LA
>*The Duplicate, Good Friends, Sweet Deal, We Are the Tits!*

"Mike Kimmel has handed the reader years' worth of knowledge in one succinct book. I have worked in Hollywood for over twenty-five years as both an actor and director, and the points the author makes are one hundred percent profound. There hasn't been one situation from the book that I never saw or had friends experience first-hand. If you are thinking of moving to Hollywood, or even if you're here already, this book will save you a lot of headaches and heartache!"

>Pat Battistini
>Actor-Director-Producer, Hoosier Daddy Films
>*Ms. Rossi, Safer at Home, Tin Can, Rebound, Tortuato, Words of Wisdom, Pushing the Boundaries, Bandwidth*

"Reading this book feels like having a trusted big brother and a seasoned industry expert by your side. Mike Kimmel has poured his heart, experience, and integrity into these pages, offering guidance that is both practical and encouraging. His ability to distill the truths of Hollywood into such thoughtful advice is a reflection of his generosity and wisdom. Mike isn't just an incredible talent—he's a mentor whose words inspire confidence and clarity for anyone chasing their dreams in this industry."

    SARA STARR
    Actor-Writer-Director
    The Bunker, The Journey Back, Last Call, The Cleaning Lady

"This is a great read! It is a must for every actor to have and refer to on a regular basis. Having this book is like having a close friend who is always with you to share a quick reminder or word of encouragement. The next best thing would be to actually have Mike Kimmel as your friend, and I consider myself blessed to call Mike a friend. Bravo, Mike!"

    LENA ARMSTRONG
    Actor-Dancer-Producer
    Law & Order, The Night Shift, The Wonderful Ice Cream Suit, Dandelion Man, Deuces Wild, Keep Your Nose Clean, Kink, Inc.

"What makes this guide stand out is its sympathetic tone. Kimmel is candid about the darker corners of Hollywood … yet he never lingers in bitterness. Instead, he balances cautionary tales with encouragement."

    SAN FRANCISCO BOOK REVIEW

"Mike never ceases to put out much-needed information for actors. This industry is not for the faint of heart and often leaves you questioning your talent, your worth and, often times, your choice of career. This book nails it! It not only gives the actor some vital nuggets about the industry, but it also eases your mind to know that whatever you're going through, others have too. Bravo, Mike!"

>April Hartman
>Actor-Producer,
>Co-Owner of Act Up Studios,
>*Reservation Dogs, Queer as Folk, The Devil's Ring, Keily, Breakers, On Becoming a God in Central Florida*

"If there was ever a no-nonsense Guide To Hollywood for actors new and old, this is it. Just one little jewel from this book of fifty could make *all* the difference in the world for you. Avoiding the pitfalls, using the best resources and truly giving you a better chance to find yourself in the incredible adventure called Hollywood, that's what this guidebook delivers.

Young or old, this book could literally give you a leg up on your career path, and knowing what *not* to do can even save your life in Hollywood. It's a truly dangerous city for the naïve.

For those already on their journey, you may find that one little thing that changes everything. For the new generation of artists coming to the bright lights of Hollywood with a dream, start here."

>Susannah Devereux
>Portrayed Dianne Neilson on *Shortland Street* for Television New Zealand,
>*Creepshow, Silver Twins, Moscow Station, The Lost Day, Confined, Heavy, Falling Down the Mountain, Second Hand Rose*

For Francis Ford Coppola,
who believed in me when I needed it most

"Someone said to me, 'If fifty percent of the experts in Hollywood said you had no talent and should give up, what would you do?' My answer was then and still is, 'If a hundred percent told me that, all one hundred percent would be wrong.'"

Marilyn Monroe

Table of Contents

Praise for *50 Secrets Nobody Tells You in Hollywood*	v
Foreword by GiGi Erneta	xix
Acknowledgments	xxiii
Introduction	xv
A Note on Self-Tapes and the Future	xxxv

1. The Best Actor Doesn't Always Get the Job	1
2. Sometimes the Answer Is "No" Before You Even Walk Through the Door	4
3. Some Will See You as a Threat	7
4. Don't Sign Across the Board	9
5. Expand Your Radius. Widen Your Circle.	12
6. Nobody Cares What You Drive	15
7. Get a Job	18
8. There Are No Small Parts	22
9. You're a Type. Know It. Own It. Nail It.	26
10. Don't Change Your Look	28
11. Don't Disqualify Yourself	30
12. Take a Stage Combat Class	34
13. Ask Them to Show You	37
14. Keep Your Shirt On	40

15. Don't Take the Bait	43
16. Don't Become a Groupie	46
17. Learn to Compartmentalize	48
18. Don't Slurp Your Soup	51
19. Two Ears. One Mouth. Do the Math.	53
20. Master the Fine Art of Listening	56
21. Not Everything Requires Your Response	59
22. You're Not a Walking Resume	61
23. Use Your Voicemail	64
24. Watch Your Language	67
25. Your Hand Can Shake You Right Out the Door	69
26. Don't Stink Up the Room	71
27. Pay Attention. Eyes Open. Head on a Swivel.	73
28. Beware the Green-Eyed Monster	76
29. Be Flexible. Be Adaptable. Be Bookable.	79
30. Theater Credits Count	82
31. Overcome Skepticism with Specificity	85
32. Be Mega-Prepared	88
33. Practice Never Makes Perfect	93
34. Think like a Producer	96
35. You Should Write Something	100
36. Get Used to Criticism. You Will Get It.	103
37. The One-Strike Rule	106
38. The Experts Aren't Always Right	110
39. Don't Be Guilty by Association	113
40. Develop Legendary Patience and Focus	116

41. Never Do Stock	119
42. Don't Ask for Coffee	122
43. Don't Badmouth Your Agent	125
44. Don't Talk About Your Health Problems	130
45. Nothing Good Happens After Midnight	133
46. Make Friends with Procrastination	135
47. Act Right	138
48. Recharge Your Battery	142
49. A Lesson from *The Duck Factory*	145
50. The Clock Is Ticking	148
Afterword: Give It Your All	153

Appendices

A Suggestion for Younger Actors	157
A Suggestion for Older Actors	160
A Challenge for Acting Teachers	165
Discussion Questions and Ideas for Further Study	170
Recommended Reading	190
A Note on Self-Care	195
About GiGi Erneta	201
About Mike Kimmel	203
A Bold and Humble Request	205

Also by Mike Kimmel

Adult

Monologues for Adults
Monologues for Young Adults
The Actor's Book of Quotes
Six Critical Essays on Film

Teen

Scenes for Teens
Monologues for Teens
Monologues for Teens II
One-Minute Monologues for Teens

Children

Acting Scenes for Kids and Tweens
Monologues for Kids and Tweens
Monologues for Kids and Tweens II

Foreword

Sitting in the waiting room, not just any waiting room, but one that I had been waiting for years to be asked into. Finally: Access Granted! Casting offices can sometimes resemble a dragon's lair in your mind. The mind can be very freeing and very frightening. There is constant dialogue when your adrenaline is moving.

Back to the waiting room.

Okay, stay calm.

Don't look at ANYBODY!

But there are people everywhere waiting to go in for the same role. And wait, she's like twenty years younger than me but I like her shoes.

The lady next to me almost looks like me, same hair, much nicer suit. Another lady with a similar look walks in, almost announcing, "I just got here from New York."

Suit lady says, "Me too. What part?"

Sit on your hands, look straight ahead and don't say a word. (I actually did that; it took every ounce of self-control I could muster. I'm from New York, too, and we like to gab.)

That is when I chose the higher ground. No, literally, I started praying. Leaned my head back against the wall, closed my eyes, and then everything that mattered came back to me—who I was, every line of dialogue, and the freedom to enjoy being one with my character.

Adrenaline was still flowing, so I admit, I peeked once, and to my dismay, another actress had walked in and was signing in right in front of me. The sign-in sheet was in front of my chair. A little too close for my comfort. You get the picture. She turned around, and I was still leaning my head back against the wall, so I quickly shut my eyes. She was mid-question when she apologized to me for interrupting my "zone." A veteran performer will acknowledge and respect that space.

Clock ticks on the wall.

"Next," said the casting director. (Much like a doctor's office.) Adrenaline charges through my veins. In my mind, I pause my oneness and think, *is it me?*

I open my eyes.

Silence.

The lady in the nice suit gets up, and I quickly close my eyes and go to that sweet spot.

I'm on "deck" as they say. So excited I can't stand it!

I'm GiGi Erneta. I'm an actress and have been for most of my life. In case you were wondering how that story ended, I booked that television show. The reason I shared it with you is because that "waiting room" exists for every actor. Whether it is an audition that is live in a building, on Zoom, or taped, things happen to actors. How they respond is the difference between victory and failure.

This wonderful book will open your eyes to many secrets that Hollywood may try keeping from you. There are gems in this book that will help you avoid the pitfalls many of us had to fall into in order to learn. Save yourself the time, kick back and enjoy the read. In this business, you will need every tool you can get your hands on; it is a battlefield. Work on your craft and learn the business. It is a business, and if you want to earn money, you better know what you are doing!

Mike Kimmel has been doing this a long time. He also teaches and has pearls of wisdom that constantly flow from him. He could probably create volumes of books with the wealth of information he has acquired over the years!

So, when you go into that audition, the one you have been waiting for, be calm and go inside yourself, become one with your material, enjoy the process. Have the information from this book in your foundation so you are armed before you go into the "dragon's lair." Study, read, practice, live, love and be the best version of you! NEVER, EVER give up on your dream, no matter what anybody says. And remember, every time you get a "no," you are one step closer to a "yes!"

GiGi Erneta
Hollywood, California

Acknowledgments

As always, a million thanks to my wonderful family—my sisters, their husbands, their children, and children's children—for always being there for me.

Many thanks to Tracey Adlai, Summer Alvarez, Holly Anderson, Lena Armstrong, Laura Cayouette, Nora Isabel Cross, Susannah Devereux, Kimber Eastwood, Sharon Garrison, Tina and A.J. Guillot, April Hartman, Valerie Marsch, Layla Milholen, Nicole Pachl, Sara Starr, Joyce Storey, Pat Battistini, Jim Blumetti, David Breland, Chuck Disney, Freddie Ganno, Christopher Jones, Ben McCain, Butch McCain, Ben Rose, and William Wellman Jr. for their friendship, encouragement, inspiration, and support throughout the writing process.

Very special thanks to my lifelong friend and colleague, GiGi Erneta, for taking the time to write the foreword to this book. GiGi is an immensely talented actor, writer, director, producer, host, and voice-over artist. She is also one of the smartest, strongest, most capable people I've ever met. I'm grateful for our many years of friendship, and look forward to many more coffees, conversations, and collaborations in the future.

> "You start where you can get an opportunity, you take everything that you can do to gain entrance. You do the little work and you try to find people who can teach you."
>
> — Jon Voight

Introduction

It's no secret that show business is an extremely competitive field. There have always been far more qualified actors in the industry than available roles for them to fill in film, television, and theater. Nevertheless, actors continue to line up for the opportunity to shine on stage and screen.

Ray Bradbury, the legendary science fiction writer, said that if we trusted our intellect alone, we would never take a chance on pursuing a new friendship, a new romantic interest, or starting a new business. The potential for loss, disappointment, and pain are simply too great.

But artists—and actors in particular—are seldom logical in pursuit of their dreams. As a group, we've been known to quit our day jobs, leave the safety and security of home and family, travel halfway around the world, and risk everything on something as ephemeral as an audition.

"If you've got theater in your blood," the old saying goes, "don't quit until your blood is all over the theater." That sounds melodramatic, of course, but drama is our business.

It's prudent, however, to work smarter rather than harder. It's important to learn the rules that govern our industry—so that we may operate safely and effectively within its guidelines, framework, and parameters.

Mike Kimmel

A Note of Thanks

Thank you for selecting this book. I wish it were available when I first touched down in Hollywood. It would have saved me many hours of stress, anxiety, frustration, uncertainty … and several truckloads of hundred-dollar bills.

There are a great many factors at play in the entertainment industry. There's a tremendous amount of money at stake, and there are many things actors traditionally have learned only through hard and bitter experience. I've learned many of the lessons in this book through my own often-painful experiences. I've also benefitted from the shared experiences of trusted friends and colleagues. Many experienced actors, writers, producers, and directors have shared their own "war stories" with me through the years—including their victories, defeats, and personal and professional challenges within our industry. Some of these faithful friends—like GiGi Erneta—have also been gracious enough to lend their time, talent, and practical experience to writing forewords for my books.

It's extremely important to have a solid support system in Hollywood—and to surround yourself with reliable, reputable, well-intentioned people whose backgrounds and ethical standards you can trust. I've been fortunate enough to meet, befriend, and collaborate with terrific performers—and professionals in many other areas of the business—through the years. As in any industry, we've all faced daily challenges and have learned to seek out advice, good judgement, and wise counsel from others in our group when faced with difficult decisions and circumstances.

We check in with one another regularly. We ask each other for advice. A typical conversation may begin with, "Okay, I guarantee you haven't heard *this one* before." The experiences we share with one another are incredibly valuable. They help all of us gain a greater understanding of the industry and its many peculiarities. We benefit from each other's experiences—both positive and negative. We've all taken our share of lumps through the years. We've also been there to remind each other of all the wins we've enjoyed along the way—and encourage one another to keep moving forward towards tomorrow's new opportunities and successes.

Wherever possible, I've sprinkled our real-life Hollywood stories throughout this book. We often learn best through stories and practical, real-world examples. My colleagues and I have tested the waters for you. We've made some brilliant choices and some embarrassing mistakes. We've won major victories and bounced back from crushing defeats. You can learn from our combined experiences—so that you don't have to reinvent the wheel (and take all the lumps) for yourself.

Because the entertainment industry is so competitive, there are many secrets and bits of advice people will be reluctant to share with you—but these can still negatively impact your ability to land an agent, book good roles, establish a solid career and reputation, and maintain your sanity here in Hollywood.

You can't win a fight you don't know you're in.

You can't win a fight you don't know you're in. Many actors in Hollywood don't know what they're up against until it's too late—and has already negatively impacted their careers. We can't do everything alone. Everyone in the entertainment industry needs guidance, training, and direction. This is true even at the highest levels in Hollywood. I've coached actors whose resumes were ten times longer than my own. Ask yourself what one hour of your time is worth. Then ask yourself what one year of your life is worth. Then ask yourself what the opportunity cost may be for failing to seek out teachers and mentors who can help you move forward towards your goals.

My Own Background and Experiences

My own actor's journey has been non-traditional at best. I was born into humble circumstances in the Bronx, New York. Opportunities were scarce back in those early days. Nobody from our neighborhood ventured far outside our neighborhood. The bright lights of Hollywood seemed light years away. Though the Broadway lights were just a one-hour subway ride from our modest family home, they might just as well have been shining on the dark side of the moon. The entire industry seemed completely inaccessible from where I was at that time. There were no acting classes or after-school programs in our community, my family didn't know anyone in the business, and I couldn't find a good starting point in the performing arts through our local schools and libraries.

Nevertheless, I knew from the time I was five years old that I wanted to perform on stage and screen, write books and scripts, and tell stories. I knew exactly what I wanted to do but had no idea how to make it happen. I also couldn't find anyone reputable to guide me. Consequently, I never had the chance to work as a child actor. I gravitated towards other interests and industries but promised myself to keep nurturing those early show biz dreams and aspirations. I also promised myself that if I were someday able to break into the industry, build my credits, and learn the ropes, I would do my best to share everything I've learned with others. We don't gain much in life from holding back.

The Reason for this Book Series

Once I began training and working regularly as an actor in my twenties, I discovered I was not alone. I connected with many other actors who shared my early confusion and uncertainty about how to break into the business—and how to learn the rules of the game. Though our backgrounds and geography were different, our experiences were remarkably similar. We eventually got started, of course, but it wasn't until many years after we would have liked to begin. Looking back, I've always wished I could have started earlier. The real value, however, in looking back is to ensure that our knowledge base is strong enough to launch us forward into the future we wish to create for ourselves and others.

Hollywood and New York—the two largest markets in the U.S. entertainment industry—are very different places with very different sets of rules and standards. Though I landed in Hollywood with respectable credits and training from New York, I still found I had a great deal to learn about the industry that was specific to the Hollywood market.

If you're an actor who lives outside Los Angeles, this book will be valuable to you, as well. If you are able to work steadily in your local market, you'll very likely work with actors from both coasts eventually. When you do, it will be extremely helpful to understand our industry from their perspective.

Mike Kimmel

The Dream Factory

Hollywood has been called the dream factory for the fortunate few who work hard to bring their own dreams into reality—or in some cases are just plain lucky. Their dreams turn into wonderful realities. For many others, unfortunately, those dreams fall by the wayside and are forgotten—or pushed forever to the back burner. In some sad cases we've seen, the dreams devolve into nightmares.

What is it that separates the successful actors from those who only achieve bit parts or only do background work throughout their entire career—and are never able to break out of that self-perpetuating cycle? A friend of mine had a nice supporting role in a Tom Cruise movie a few years ago and found himself looking back-and-forth between Mr. Cruise and his stand-in, a background player who closely resembled the star. They were about the same age, about the same size, and about the same physical type. My friend wondered to himself: "Why *him* ... and why not *him*?"

> **My friend wondered to himself: "Why *him* ... and why not *him*?"**

Is there a magic formula for success in show business? Some people will tell you it's luck. It's your look. It's who you know. It's about connections. It's about being in the right place at the right time. Maybe it's about the casting couch.

Others will tell you we become what we think about. We create our own destinies. It's all about the grind. It's all about the hustle and hard work. It's all about creating your own projects. It's all about getting yourself out there, meeting people, and networking. It's all about being in acting class twice a week.

I'm here to tell you that it's all of the above. All these opinions are true and valid—and can work in our favor to a certain extent. And there's another factor to consider, as well: how to learn (and follow) the rules of the game. Hollywood is its own unique animal—unique in all the world. It's like no other place you will ever visit. People travel here from all over the globe to make their mark in the entertainment industry.

No, I can't promise that this book will make you a star, but I can guarantee that the advice we'll cover can help you avoid some of the most common industry traps and pitfalls that have sabotaged careers in Hollywood for decades—ever since the early days of silent film. We'll also offer many strategies to help you build your credits and advance your career.

A Word of Caution … and Preparation

Baby steps.

One of the biggest mistakes I've seen actors make is moving to Los Angeles (or any larger market) too soon—and without proper training and credits. Yes, it's important to get here and start networking (and working) as quickly as you can, but it's even more important to do as much good local work as you can in your home town before jumping into the Hollywood market—the most competitive market in the world.

Even if you live in a very small town, there is likely a good-sized city with a community of actors within one hundred miles of your front door. There will be a theater community, other local actors, and acting teachers you can find. There will be local filmmakers, student filmmakers—in college and even high school—who are highly motivated to do better-than-local work. There will also be advertising agencies shooting local commercials, print advertisements, radio spots, and training films for businesses in those larger cities. There will be local talent agencies representing actors for roles in these projects. You can—and should—connect with all these people in your home market before venturing out West.

Theodore Roosevelt said it best: "Do what you can, with what you have, where you are." It's always a good idea to gain as much experience as you can locally—where the competition is less rigorous and more manageable. If you can arrive in Hollywood with a reasonable understanding of the business and decent local credits, footage, training, and audition skills from your home town, then you will be much better prepared to compete for larger projects in Los Angeles.

Optimism vs. Pessimism

I'm sometimes pessimistic about the obstacles, landmines, and uncertainty actors must face in Hollywood. However, I'm always optimistic about our ability to overcome these challenges, build a solid base, develop a reliable support system, work regularly in television, film, theater, commercials, voice-overs, hosting, and print—and enjoy a fabulous, long-term career while protecting our hearts, our souls, and our sanity.

Overall, I'm still an optimist. There's good reason for my optimism. I believe we all have a far greater capacity for success and achievement than we think we do. This is not mere positive thinking. This is accurate thinking. Success leaves visible clues. It's logical and reasonable to conclude that if another actor has accomplished something you admire in this industry, then you can do equally well if you stay focused, apply yourself diligently, and learn the Hollywood rules. I believe this book will help you get there.

My purpose in writing this book is to give you a common sense perspective, a little bit of tough love, and a full dose of reality. The advice is practical. What you choose to do with it is up to you. I hope you use these fifty secrets to help you win. I'll repeat myself at times. That's intentional. There are things we need to hear more than once. Some points need to be emphasized to support more than one of the ideas in this book. There will be some overlap. I'd rather repeat myself than under-explain something that I know is going to help you.

Stay strong. Stay focused. Stay committed to your craft—and your business. Acting is not a standard career path. Our path requires courage, discipline, intelligence, persistence, creativity, and an incredibly thick skin. I've always felt there's something noble and heroic about pursuing your show business dream—no matter what the odds may tell you. Ask yourself what would your life be like—and what would our world be like—if everyone on this planet pursued their lifelong dreams with energy, focus, and enthusiasm.

As artists, we must follow our hearts—but let's remember to take our heads with us. Your head will keep you on track. I wish you all the very best on your show business journey—and every other journey you will take in life.

Now go get 'em.

MIKE KIMMEL
LOS ANGELES, CALIFORNIA

> "People who don't think about the future don't have one."
>
> — GENE LEBELL

A Note on Self-Tapes and the Future

I began working on this book many years ago—well before the onset of the pandemic. While most of the advice relates to strategy, mindset, personal development, and work ethic, several of the chapters deal specifically with in-person auditions. Most working actors, however, have been to very few live auditions since 2020.

Actors have become extremely comfortable (and proficient) with self-tapes. Producers, directors, and casting directors are able to save time and money with the new technology. They can now see more actors per role in a shorter period of time. Many independent casting directors have given up their office spaces and now work primarily from home. It's hard to imagine these same casting directors renting out new office spaces after becoming so comfortable and efficient working with the new technology in the privacy of their homes.

For these reasons, most of my colleagues feel that in-person auditions are largely a thing of the past. I disagree. While I believe that self-tapes are here to stay, I also feel that in-person auditions will never go away completely. In fact, I believe that live auditions—especially in Los Angeles, New York, Chicago, Austin, and New Orleans—will come back to a far greater extent than we're seeing now.

It's difficult to predict the future. Our industry has experienced major changes several times. In the 1930s, many silent film stars were unable to keep working when sound technology was introduced. Their voices didn't match their on-screen personas. The 1950s saw a change from a more subdued and presentational style of acting to the gritty realism of Marlon Brando, James Dean, Shirley MacLaine, Shirley Booth, and others. In the 1970s, we saw the rise of indie film production. Some of the greatest films of all time were created in the 1970s—outside the traditional Hollywood studio system. Video technology in the 1990s allowed films to be produced far more inexpensively than ever before. The terrific indie feature *Laws of Gravity* was made for only $38,000—and made a star out of Peter Greene. This film's jumpy handheld camera technique influenced countless film and TV directors—and was eagerly embraced on NBC's *Law and Order*. History teaches us that change is inevitable in all industries.

Actors need to be prepared for anything. Actors in Los Angeles should always be ready to audition in person. In Hollywood, many commercials are still cast in person. More importantly, the major film studios and television networks—unlike independent casting directors—will not likely be giving up their office spaces anytime soon. Auditions for larger and recurring roles in television and film are still often held in person. Series regular roles will almost always be cast in person. There are certain intangible elements in the casting process that are difficult to convey electronically.

In recent years, as well, many productions have been burned when actors submitting self-tapes misrepresented their city of residence so that they can present themselves as local hires. Please don't say you're in one city if you're really not—or if you're not *one hundred percent sure* you can get yourself there for the scheduled days of filming. A production that has been burned by a no-show actor will be much more likely to insist on in-person auditions next time around.

For all these reasons, I believe the future will find Hollywood actors auditioning both on tape and in person. I predict it will eventually be fifty-fifty. It may take a while to get there, but I believe that's where the industry is headed. It's a good idea to prepare ourselves and become equally comfortable with both options.

Actors have to be ready for the unexpected. We must be strong enough, smart enough, and fluid enough to handle whatever the industry throws our way. We need to bring our A-game to every audition, interview, and opportunity. My good friend Jim Blumetti—a highly respected actor, audition coach, and author—calls this "releasing the Kraken."

We must be able to build upon the skill set we've spent years developing—and always be ready to change with the tides. The best actors I know prepare themselves—and are ready for anything. They never get rattled in the audition room or the Zoom room. They adapt to each new challenge, give it their all, and keep moving forward like strong, reliable, confident, seasoned, hard-working professionals. Professionals don't complain and never make excuses. They master the processes and do the hard work.

They release the Kraken.

"You've got to think of things as an opportunity.
An audition's an opportunity to have an audience."
AL PACINO

1. The Best Actor Doesn't Always Get the Job

> "I was up for a great part, but they told me, 'Sorry, you're the best actor, but this part calls for a guy-next-door type. You don't look as if you've ever lived next door to anyone.'"
>
> DONALD SUTHERLAND

It's a fact of life in Hollywood that the best actor doesn't always get the job. There are plenty of times when an actor absolutely knocks it out of the park, does an incredible audition, is physically perfect for the part—and still does not win the role.

Our industry is a qualitative—rather than quantitative—field. What this means for actors is that many decisions involving our performances are highly subjective. There are a great many variables involved in casting every role. There are many reasons we're not aware of why an actor doesn't get the job—even when that actor seems to be the best qualified. Many of these reasons cannot even be verbalized. I once heard a casting director explain: "He's just not the guy."

This is not fair, but it's a long-standing, practical reality of our industry.

However, I've seen this principle work in both directions. The converse is equally true. For all the reasons we may be overlooked, there are also occasions when we'll book a role we're not quite right for—even on days when we're not auditioning at our very best. The reasons *why we don't get a job* often make no sense. Fortunately, the reasons *why we do book the job* also sometimes make no sense.

I have an old friend, Eddie, whose career took a downturn several years ago. He hadn't booked an acting job in quite some time. Then, seemingly out of nowhere, he booked a very nice role (and a very big paycheck) on a national network commercial. It was a two-day shoot, and Eddie wanted to make the most of that opportunity. He was smart about it. He had a plan. On the second day of filming, he waited for an opportune time—when everything was going well—and then asked the director privately, "What was it about my audition that helped me book this part?" Eddie wanted to know so he could duplicate those good results in the future.

He was stunned when the director replied, "I really liked your profile. You have a very unusual profile."

Should we all go home and work on our profiles? Of course not. But this is one of my favorite Hollywood stories and a great reminder of how seemingly random considerations can also work in our favor. I can't say this is an exact science or that it works one hundred percent of the time. But I've seen it work often enough in practice to recognize this: Random events can work in our favor, even when high-paying roles are at stake.

Random events can work in our favor, even when high-paying roles are at stake.

I believe there's a deeper lesson to be learned here too—a lesson of persistence in the midst of circumstances that are wildly out of our control. Even though Eddie hadn't booked an acting job *in several years*, he never quit the business. He was frustrated and demoralized at times, but he never gave up. He stayed in the game because he truly loved this industry and always considered himself an actor—whether he was working or not.

> **"You can't always be in the reaping stage or the harvest stage of life. Life has seasons."**
> EMMA WATSON

2. Sometimes the Answer Is "No" Before You Even Walk Through the Door

"When things go wrong, don't go with them."
ELVIS PRESLEY

It's not personal. It may have nothing to do with you. And it doesn't matter how talented, great-looking, perfectly suited and well-prepared you may be for this role or this office. Sometimes the answer is "No" before you even walk through the door. Sometimes, the audition is just a formality. There are several possible explanations for this.

In television, things move very quickly. When you book a role on a TV show, you will generally shoot that episode within the next couple of weeks. In feature films, things move much more slowly. Movie producers, during the pre-production stages, are getting the lead actors to sign on, hiring the crew, nailing down locations, and securing financing.

You may audition for a film, knock it out of the park, and never find out that the financing fell through. That film can disappear for a while. In the meantime, you may think to yourself, "Oh, man. I bombed on that audition. I didn't book it or even get a callback." In reality, though, the film is still pending. You're just not seeing any forward movement because the producers have lost their money source and are trying to get new financing in place. You might hear back from their casting director six months later to "re-audition" for the same role you thought you didn't get.

Don't give up on a movie audition too quickly. Don't be so fast to write it off. While you're stressing over the choices you made in your reading, and beating yourself up for wearing the blue shirt instead of the black shirt, the producers may be scrambling to put all the pieces of the puzzle together—so they can get the money to hire you.

Another possibility is that the role may have already been "offered out" to someone else—usually a star-name actor or a solid working actor with very strong credits. Most actors who achieve a certain level of success in their careers will no longer audition for roles. They will only field offers. Those actors (and their agents) will pick and choose among offers that are presented to them.

While the producers are waiting for decisions from these actors, however, they still need to hold auditions. They need to know they can fill the role in the event their first choice actor turns it down. If their first choice decides to pass on this role, then you're still in the running. You can still book the job. However, if the more experienced actor decides to accept their offer, then every other actor who auditioned for that part is automatically rejected.

You can have the best audition of your career for a role that is not even available.

What this means is simple, but it hurts like hell. You can have the best audition of your career for a role that is not even available. The good news is that the casting director may remember you for another part in the same project—or for another project they're doing later.

Another—and slightly more sinister—explanation is also possible. The role is already booked, but the other actor's agent is battling it out with the producers over money, name billing, back-end royalties, and any other elements that are on the table in high-end contract negotiations. If these negotiations turn ugly, the producers—as a bargaining tactic—may hold auditions to show the other actor's agent they're preparing to replace his client with someone new. In this case, as well, you might audition for this role, knock it out of the park, and never know that the role you're reading for was not even available.

These situations are absolutely maddening. They can make you feel like giving up. Don't give up. More importantly, don't worry about your feelings—particularly when it comes to auditions. Nobody cares how the actor feels. Get back to work. Knock it out of the park again—and even stronger—on your next audition. Do even better next time. Make that your new habit. That's a fantastic takeaway (and true poetic justice) from doing amazing, memorable work in those situations where the odds are hopelessly stacked against you.

> **"I always look at auditions as not even getting the job as much as I'm just trying to connect with this casting director so they remember me for next time."**
> **SEBASTIAN STAN**

3. Some Will See You as a Threat

"The best revenge is massive success."
Frank Sinatra

Some talent agents will see you as a threat to clients they already represent. Don't let yourself be manipulated—and then buried in their files. As much as we should be loyal to our agent and manager allies, it's equally important to be wary of representatives who do not have our best interests in mind.

There are agents who will seek out and sign actors they perceive to be in direct competition with successful actors already on their roster. You may be very similar to an actor who books jobs regularly for a certain talent agency. An agent there might then want to sign you to their roster as well, but only to bury you in their files. Once they sign you, they'll never send you out on any auditions—so that you never have a chance to compete against their favorite client.

This is called "shelving," because they're taking you out of the marketplace and "putting you on the shelf." Some agencies who operate this way will even send you out on a limited basis to keep you happy for a while—and give the appearance that they're actually working for you.

In reality, though, they might only send you out for smaller roles that their favorite actor is not interested in playing. They may even send you out for meatier roles from time to time, but only when their favorite actor—the one they're protecting—is unavailable or already booked out on another project.

This is a particularly dirty trick that has been practiced for many years in Hollywood (and New York). It catches a lot of up-and-coming actors unawares. By the time they realize what's happening to them, they've already lost several months of audition opportunities.

Through the years, I've heard industry people say that this is only a myth. "Shelving doesn't really happen," they say. "People who talk about it are just being paranoid—and making excuses for underperforming." When I was first starting out, though, I had an agent in a very small office who had worked for one of the "Big Three" agencies for most of her thirty-plus year career. She once confided to me that shelving was a very common practice among all of the agents at her former mega-office. They all did it—and it was actively encouraged at the highest levels of management.

A good rule of thumb is to give the relationship with any new agent or manager three to six months to test the waters. You might think of this as your "honeymoon period." Trust your gut during this trial period. If you feel that your new agent isn't working hard on your behalf within those first few months—and if you start to notice any red flags—it's possible that your new representative may actually be working against you.

> "I'd rather be rejected than used because they both amount to the same thing in the end, but being used takes a lot longer."
>
> MARILYN VOS SAVANT

4. Don't Sign Across the Board

"Career diversification ain't a bad thing."
VIN DIESEL

Many agents in the larger offices will insist that you "sign across the board." This means that they want to represent you in all areas of the business—television, film, commercials, print, voice-over, and hosting—everything. That's a good thing, right? Maybe. Though this strategy works well for celebrities, I think it's a bad idea for newcomers.

When you're new in town, there's a temptation to say "Yes" to everything that's offered to you. Many actors get very excited when they find they've attracted the attention of a reputable agent in a good-sized Los Angeles office. Most large agencies will insist on exclusivity. On the surface, it sounds great. "I'm covered in all areas under one roof—every medium. That's a good thing."

There's a drawback, as well. I have a friend who's a solid, consistent booker in commercials. She has probably booked more commercials than anyone I've ever known. She supported herself for years with commercial jobs and their massive residual checks. When she moved to Los Angeles, she signed across the board with a much bigger, far more prestigious office than she had worked with in her home market.

She started auditioning and booking commercials here—just as she had always done back home. That sounds like great news—and it is. Most actors would say she had nothing to complain about. What my friend really wanted, though, was to start working in film and episodic TV. That's why she moved to Hollywood in the first place. Though she had good representation (on paper) for film and TV, that department rarely sent her out on auditions.

What my friend didn't realize was that her film and television reps were reluctant to submit her for auditions because she was doing so well for the agency commercially. She was bringing in a tremendous amount of revenue, and the film and television agents didn't want to rock the boat and take her out of the commercial pool. The reasoning is that if they booked her on an episodic television job, she might be unavailable for a (better paying) commercial job with the agent across the hall.

In situations like this, we have to remember that both departments are working for the same office. The department with the lower-paying job will be very reluctant to pull my friend away from another department where she is making big money. Nobody wants to kill the golden goose.

Agents don't always have *our long-term interests* in mind when submitting us for auditions.

The takeaway from this example is: Agents don't always have *our long-term interests in mind* when submitting us for auditions. My friend's agents were more interested in the immediate payday in the area where she was most likely to perform well: commercials. This is not the case for all agents, of course. There are agents and managers out there who will partner with you and help you to strategize and reinvent yourself. It's a tricky subject. This is not an exact science, but I know my friend would have been much happier signing with a variety of agents in several different offices—one for each different area of our business.

It's a nice status symbol to have a prestigious agency name on our resumes. Ironically, though, she didn't even need to be with a top-tier agency commercially. With her audition skills and long list of commercial credits, my friend had tons of other options. There are dozens of small and mid-sized commercial agencies that would have been salivating to have her on their list.

It would have been better for my friend's career (and her mindset) to connect with an aggressive, hungry agent at a smaller office specializing in film and episodic TV—someone who believed in her, saw dollar signs, and would work hard to get her in the door for the type of projects she moved here to shoot. Once she had that part of the Hollywood puzzle solved, she could then meet with commercial agents in other offices and select one that she felt would be a good personality match.

That's why my advice to Hollywood newcomers is not to sign across the board. The exception is when a new actor is booking successfully in one area—and is not terribly interested in other types of projects. In that case, any bookings or publicity opportunities in other areas would just be icing on the cake. Signing across the board also works well for celebrities with well-established careers. Most working actors and newcomers, though, can multiply their opportunities by signing with agents in several different offices—one for each different area of the business.

> **"I think one of the things that saved me is that I never put all my eggs in one basket."**
> **R**ICKY **S**CHROEDER

5. Expand Your Radius. Widen Your Circle.

> "I am not a product of my circumstances.
> I am a product of my decisions."
> **STEPHEN COVEY**

Sometimes actors need to widen their circle and expand their reach. This is a technique perfected by the most successful actors in smaller markets across the country. Hollywood actors can benefit from this strategy as well.

We're not trees. We don't have to remain where we've been planted. If you can't find enough acting work—and enough good opportunities—in Los Angeles, where competition is the fiercest, then it may be worth your while to start traveling to adjoining markets where the competition is not quite so rigorous.

For many years, I had agents in Orange County and San Diego—and auditioned regularly in those two markets. I did the same thing when I was starting out in New York. I had agents in Connecticut, New Jersey, and Philadelphia. The jobs were a little smaller. The pay was a little bit less. The travel, admittedly, was sometimes a hassle. But I could usually book three or four of those gigs each year in the smaller markets. Success breeds success. Booking in a smaller market is good for your head and wallet—and can do wonders for your self-esteem. From Los Angeles, you can expand north to San Francisco, Oregon, and

Success breeds success. Booking in a smaller market is good for your head and wallet—and can do wonders for your self-esteem.

Washington, south to San Diego and Orange County, and east to Nevada, Arizona, Colorado, Utah, New Mexico, and Texas.

The good news is that with the rise of self-taping, actors can now audition for jobs across the country without stepping outside the front door. If you book the role, of course, you'll have to travel to where the job is filming to shoot it—usually at your own expense.

This can be rough on your body and your budget. Driving long distances for auditions, callbacks and jobs is exhausting and expensive. Many performers, however, start booking far more work once they make the decision to become "road warriors." Many working pros have this process down to a science and are incredibly good at it. They build relationships with casting directors, agents, directors, and producers in many different cities. They always have their bags packed. They always have a full tank of gas. They always have frequent flyer miles they can redeem. They're always ready to get in the car (or hop on a plane) at a moment's notice.

I wouldn't say it's an easy lifestyle—especially if you're married. But I've known actors who became extremely frustrated through the years—feeling they had gone as far as they could in the city where they were based. Instead of giving up and quitting the business, their frustration impelled them into positive and productive activity.

These dedicated actors started to achieve far greater success once they made the decision to set out on the open road and increase their number of "available at bats" by auditioning in multiple markets across the country. I recently worked with an actor who told me she puts one hundred thousand miles on her car every year. While this is extreme, it's not at all surprising. It's simply another example of the extraordinary commitment solid working actors bring to their careers every day of the year. Author and entrepreneur Tim Ferriss said it best: "You always have options. You may just not like those options."

> **"I couldn't wait for success, so I went ahead without it."**
> JONATHAN WINTERS

6. Nobody Cares What You Drive

"Beware of over-concern for money, or position, or glory. Someday you will meet a man who cares for none of these things. Then you will know how poor you are."
Rudyard Kipling

I coached an actor years ago who planned to move to Hollywood with a group of friends from his hometown. His friends all moved here together. They shared a house rental and were extremely helpful to one another when they arrived. Little by little, they all got settled, got agents, and got started. This young man delayed his move several times so that he could save enough money to buy a flashy luxury car.

He explained that he needed an expensive car because he wanted industry folks to know he was successful as soon as they met him. I didn't have the heart to tell him that when we arrive at in-person auditions in Hollywood, there's usually a posted sign that reads, "No Actor Parking." Actors normally park a couple of blocks away. Even after the audition, when we're booked on speaking roles in TV and film, our designated parking area is generally located a short distance from the filming location. We then take a shuttle van to set.

Don't try to impress people with your car. The people you want to impress may never even see it. If you're a car enthusiast and it makes you feel good to drive a fancy one, then by all means treat yourself to something nice that you can afford. But don't overextend yourself with payments you can't afford to impress strangers.

Let me provide some context. A well-known Hollywood producer reportedly received a settlement of more than two hundred million dollars from his former studio when they parted ways. Afterwards, he continued driving the same car he had driven for several years—a Ford Mustang. Clearly, he could afford any car on the planet, but didn't feel the need to impress others with his flashy ride.

One thing millionaires and billionaires seem to have in common is that they don't throw money around unnecessarily. Maybe that's why they're millionaires and billionaires. They'll be generous when the mood strikes them, but they don't spend money lavishly just because they can. They don't feel the need to impress strangers. They have nothing to prove. Jack Benny said it best: "A rich man is one who isn't afraid to ask the salesperson to show him something cheaper."

If you'd like to see a practical example of this for yourself, take a drive out to the Huntington Gardens Library and Museum in San Marino, near Pasadena. It's an attraction that is well worth seeing, and probably one of the most beautiful places in California. It might be one of the most beautiful places in the world. The museum is situated in a wealthy community among palatial, multi-million dollar estates. Interestingly, however, you'll see mostly older model cars parked in the driveways. Nothing flashy. Apparently, these residents know the value of a dollar and like to keep track of those dollars. Many wealthy people exercise caution as well, knowing that driving expensive vehicles can make them targets for carjackers, scammers, and opportunists.

Please don't buy things you can't afford. People spend money they don't have to buy things they don't need to impress people who don't care. This is a common trap that has, unfortunately, sabotaged countless careers in Hollywood. Avoid racking up unnecessary debt. I've seen it create needless stress, turmoil, and anxiety for so many smart, talented actors through the years. I've seen it end some very promising careers too.

The poet Ezra Pound shared a powerful and thought-provoking message on this topic. "Wars in old times were made to get slaves," Pound wrote. "The modern implement of imposing slavery is debt."

Learn to impress people with your audition skills, work ethic, intelligence, creativity, personal integrity, and the way you treat others. In the long run, you'll make a far more lasting impression.

> **"A man is rich in proportion to the things he can afford to let alone."**
> **HENRY DAVID THOREAU**

7. Get a Job

> *"Don't sit around doing nothing, spending your nest egg. Get some income, so you can save the nest egg and only spend little bits of it when necessary. If you have money coming in, you can use your nest egg to supplement times when you must quit your day job in order to take a low-paying acting job."*
>
> — JENNA FISCHER

Get a job and be productive. There's no shame in waiting tables, tending bar, substitute teaching, driving a limo, or any of the other myriad survival jobs actors have traditionally held through the years. There's something wrong, however, in believing that you're "above" these type of jobs and "too good" for any kind of work outside the entertainment industry because you are now officially an "artiste."

A variety of oddball jobs can do wonders for your creativity as an actor—and give you plenty of good material to draw upon when prepping for auditions. Allison Tolman said it best: "If you only live in the world of the actor, and if you only live in the world of auditions, etc., then you don't really have a whole lot to offer when it comes to playing the humans that you're trying to audition for."

Get a job—and be open to learning all the life lessons that job will teach you. Method actors do this all the time, by the way. Robert DeNiro drove a cab in New York City when prepping for his breakout role in *Taxi Driver*. He had just finished shooting *Godfather II* in Italy. I'm pretty sure he didn't need the cash.

In a practical sense, though, it's important to build—and maintain—a solid nest egg to protect yourself from the inevitable ups and downs of our industry. I've known so many actors through the years, unfortunately, who were so busy scrambling to meet their bills each month that they were never able to devote their best efforts to their acting careers. They were always trying to catch up financially. Keeping a steady stream of money coming in provides long-term peace of mind—and allows you to focus on the reason you moved here. Gene Autry, the famous singing cowboy, called this "keeping your line of supply open."

Many Hollywood actors prefer to juggle several different part-time jobs so they're protected in case one of their income sources dries up. That's what I started doing when I arrived in Hollywood. I first worked as a security guard on the night shift. Later, I became certified to teach classes in adult education in the public school system. Most adult school classes were in the evening, so I had my days free for auditions. On the weekends, I performed in murder mystery shows, did a magic act for children's birthday parties, and made balloon animals table-to-table in a restaurant. I used to joke that if anyone broke into my apartment back in those days, they'd be scared to death. They'd find my headshots and resumes, security uniform and badge, school books and ID cards, magic props, balloon animals, and the costumes for the murder mystery dinner theater shows. They would think ten different people lived in that apartment—and turn around and run for their lives!

All of this was a juggling act for sure, but it was super-exciting for me at the same time. Once I started booking acting work here, I could let go of a couple of those jobs. Believe it or not, though, I loved every one of my survival jobs at the time. I didn't dread going to work, I loved it. I was happy knowing that I had finally arrived in Hollywood—where I had always wanted to be—and was one hundred percent self-sufficient. I was pursuing my dream with no excuses—and without being a burden on anyone. I was happy that I didn't have to borrow money to move here or stay here—and that I was being careful to maintain a little financial cushion each month. The creativity that makes us good actors can also help us become more financially resourceful—and find imaginative ways to stay afloat during the inevitable ups and downs of our industry.

Whatever you do to make money, though, please make sure your job allows some flexibility for auditions. Flexibility for auditions is vital. This is not up for debate. Your agent will be furious if you turn down an audition or booking because you can't take time off from your survival job. That's one of an agent's pet peeves, by the way. Through the years, several agents have told me they will drop a client the very first time that client turns down an audition because of scheduling. No exceptions. No second chances.

From an actor's perspective, that may sound harsh. From an agent's perspective, though, they're busting their tails trying to get us in the door for auditions—and then we turn around and

---

Flexibility for auditions is vital. This is not up for debate. Your agent will be furious if you turn down an audition or booking because you can't take time off from your survival job.

tell them we're not available. It makes us look flaky, irresponsible, and unable to manage our finances and our lives. Worse yet, it makes us appear ungrateful to our agents for all their efforts and hard work on our behalf.

Whatever your financial picture—and even if you don't need the money—I would still encourage you to get a part-time job (or a volunteer position) where you can be productive, contribute to the California economy, and feel like you're part of the local workforce.

An outside job will give you an opportunity to meet people and make friends outside your normal circle. It will broaden you, give you a little perspective, sharpen your skills, help you with time management—and remind you of the value of a dollar. It will keep you from worrying about whether your money will last through the end of the month. Best of all, it will get you out of your apartment … and out of your head.

> "I worked at Deutsche Bank for about eight years on their overnight shift. I was working consistently in the theater. I just wanted to know that my rent was going to be paid on time."
> CHANDRA WILSON

8. There Are No Small Parts

"A good writer—and I think it's this way with actors too—even if you have two lines, you have to do the same complete work as if you're number one on the call sheet. If you get in an elevator and somebody gets on, rides two floors and gets off, that person has a reality that goes back to when they were born. They have memories, they have people, they have a life. They are doing something right now that the camera is on them in their space. We live in our own close-up all the time."

ALFRE WOODARD

There are no small parts, only small actors. That's an oldie, but still a goodie.

My friend and colleague Laura Cayouette wrote a terrific book on this subject. *Know Small Parts* is the definitive guide to helping actors make the most of the smaller roles that frequently come our way. This usually happens early in one's career, but it's not uncommon for actors with many years of experience and major roles behind them to continue performing smaller-than-normal roles from time to time. We've even seen major stars appear in minor roles—like Matt Damon in *Thor: Ragnarok*, Robert Duvall in *Sling Blade*, and Liv Tyler in *U Turn*.

The trick is to give your full attention to that one-day role, to make that one-day role the most important thing in the world to you. Too many actors spend their time on set complaining about

Total commitment should always be our goal, no matter how many lines the screenwriter or playwright gave us.

their present roles and reminiscing about how wonderful their previous opportunities have been. This is definitely the wrong approach—and will not win you many friends on set.

Your creativity and imagination do not begin and end on the printed page. Flesh out your characters. Actors must learn how to use their creative energies to throw themselves fully into every role they inhabit. This is known as "total commitment to the part." Total commitment should always be our goal, no matter how many lines the screenwriter or playwright gave us.

The novelist Ford Madox Ford explained this principle from a literary perspective. "If you're going to have a character appear in a story long enough to sell a newspaper," the author explained, "he'd better be real enough that you can smell his breath." The size of the role is irrelevant. It's the actor's job to breathe life into those supporting characters on stage and screen.

Early in my career, I performed in a stage play at Equity Library Theatre in New York with an older gentleman named Bob Horen. Bob had a long, successful career spanning more than five decades in theater, film, television, and commercials. He wasn't a star, but he worked regularly from his twenties through his seventies. Backstage one night, Bob told me about his first Broadway role in the Big Apple as a young twenty-something. He played a Western Union foot messenger, delivering a telegram to one of the lead characters in the play. I believe he had one or two lines late in the third act of a large-scale Broadway production. It was a tiny role.

During the run of that show, when Bob's friends would ask what the play was about, he would answer: "Well, it's about this Western Union messenger boy. He's the focal point. He's the lynchpin of the entire play. He has this real important, life-changing message to deliver to the star of the show. Every scene in the play has built up to this point. Everybody's on pins and needles waiting for him. The whole cast is on stage waiting for my character to arrive in Act Three, deliver this important message, and save the day."

"Meanwhile, my guy is praying he'll get a good tip. He got stiffed on his last four deliveries tonight. He's worried now because his rent is due at the little flophouse down in the Bowery where he rents a room. If he doesn't make his rent this week, the manager, Old Man McGillicutty, is gonna kick him out. McGillicutty has been on a rampage all week. He's drinking again. He's out of control. He has it in for my guy. The pressure is on. So what I do to prepare myself before knocking on this door tonight is …"

Get the picture? Bob Horen had the right idea. He created a rich, full backstory for this very small role he was so happy to have booked early in his career. He created a vivid image in his mind of the entire play from the point of view of the Western Union foot messenger. All these years later, I can still see Old Man McGillicutty waiting for Bob with a sour look on his face, holding a big, hairy hand out for his overdue rent money.

That messenger boy role may have been a bit part to the playwright, but it was a very big deal to Bob. Maybe that's why he

---
He created a rich, full backstory for this very small role he was so happy to have booked early in his career.
---

worked steadily in our industry for fifty years. Let's honor Bob Horen's memory today by following his example. Be grateful for every opportunity, no matter how small. Put everything you've got into everything you do. Make every role your masterpiece.

> "I was in Woody Allen's *Stardust Memories* in 1980. It was only a bit part, and I didn't get to speak, but I felt that I was in a real movie and heading where I had always wanted to be."
>
> SHARON STONE

9. You're a Type. Know It. Own It. Nail It.

> *"I'd played dumbasses a lot. On Mad About You, I played a very dumb waitress and they saw me."*
> LISA KUDROW

Is Woody Allen a romantic leading man? In a Woody Allen film, the answer is "Yes." Outside of his own projects, however, most people wouldn't see him that way. This is not a criticism of Mr. Allen or his films. I'm a native New Yorker and a big fan of his work—but I believe that few other directors would cast him in the same way he casts himself.

Most actors pride themselves on having a broad range. We like to think we can play a wider range, in fact, than we usually can. It's easier to do that in theater because we can use heavy makeup and props—and the audience is far away. Television and film are much less forgiving. The camera doesn't lie. While it's important for actors not to limit ourselves (Secret 11: Don't Disqualify Yourself), it's even more important to understand *how we are most likely to be cast*.

While it's important for actors not to limit ourselves ... it's even more important to understand *how we are most likely to be cast*.

It's important to know ourselves and the type of roles we are most likely to play. You should have headshots and a few wardrobe choices that show you off well in those roles. It would be a good idea to have a monologue or two that represents you well for those characters.

I remember an interview with Dennis Franz right after he booked the role of Andy Sipowicz on *Law and Order*. The reporter asked how it felt to play another cop—after he had just finished a long-running police officer role on *Hill Street Blues*. Mr. Franz said that it felt the same as it did to play the last fifty cops throughout his career. The reporter, of course, was just commenting on his two most recent, most visible, and highest-paid police officer roles.

Dennis Franz knows his type—rough-edged, hard-drinking, gritty urban cops and detectives who aren't above bending the rules (and roughing up a suspect). He has been playing characters like this for most of his career. He understands his type and became super-successful by embracing it. We would all do well to follow his example. Be willing to stretch and play characters that are very different from our norm when given the opportunity—but learn to recognize (and embrace) the way in which we are *most likely* to be cast. We have to know ourselves well to pitch ourselves well.

> **"My only problem is finding a way to play my fortieth fallen female in a different way from my thirty-ninth."**
> BARBARA STANWYCK

10. Don't Change Your Look

> *"You know when you're young and you see a play in high school, and the guys all have gray in their hair and they're trying to be old men and they have no idea what that's like? It's just that stupid the other way around."*
>
> CLINT EASTWOOD

It's normal to want to change our appearance from time to time. We're human, and there's nothing wrong with actors wanting to experiment with all the tools nature gave us to work with. We all want to look our best.

Remember, though, that once your agents and managers—and the casting directors, directors, and producers who can hire you—get used to seeing you with a certain look or style—that visual image becomes part of your personal "brand." Be careful not to surprise your industry colleagues by showing up with a totally different look than they're accustomed to seeing on your headshots, marketing materials, and online casting profiles.

Our agents and managers are busy marketing us with a certain look, so make sure you're always on the same page. Make sure you're working together as a team with your representatives for the common good. You all have the same goals: getting you seen, getting you booked, and getting you paid. It's a team effort. Always make sure your look is consistent so you're never operating at cross-purposes with your representation.

Always make sure your look is consistent so you're never operating at cross-purposes with your representation.

For example, I've carried some extra weight around the middle for most of my career. My weight has gone up. My weight has gone down. Generally speaking, though, *my type* has not changed.

Some years ago, I became interested in starting a strict health regimen, dropping some pounds, and really whipping myself into better shape. I wasn't trying to make the Olympic team; I just wanted to look and feel better. I met with my agent at the time and told him my plans. I expected a little resistance, but that was not his response. My agent liked the idea, and explained that if I dropped the weight, he could start submitting me for fast food commercials. (Think about it. We seldom see plus-sized talent in fast food commercials.)

What my agent liked best, I think, was that I took the time to schedule an in-person meeting, tell him my ideas, and ask his advice. Always remember that we're in the communications industry. Good communication with our team members is vitally important for long-term success.

> "The greatest communication skill is paying value to others."
> **Denis Waitley**

11. Don't Disqualify Yourself

"The most exciting acting tends to happen in roles you never thought you could play."
JOHN LITHGOW

While it's important to know how we are most likely to be cast, we should understand that age range and physical type are often flexible. It's important never to disqualify ourselves.

Over the years, I've seen actors talk themselves out of auditioning for roles they might have otherwise booked. The two most common areas in which actors disqualify themselves are their age and physical type.

Don't let yourself get locked into too narrow an age range. Roles and scripts intended for a particular age are easily adapted for actors whose performances pique our interest—and merit closer consideration. Very often, in fact, the dialogue only needs a slight adaptation or modification to suit the age range of the newly considered actor. Sometimes, the script does not need to be changed at all—not even a single word.

Most actors who have been around the block are accustomed to playing roles several years younger—and older—than their actual chronological ages. This has been common knowledge and practice in Hollywood for decades.

For example, I've written several scene and monologue books for children and teenagers. With slight modifications, I later used much of this material in classes for adult actors in their twenties, thirties, forties—and beyond. Several colleges and universities have done the same. They've added my younger-themed books to their university libraries and the academic course reserves for their theater and film programs.

> **Start thinking of age as a general guideline created by writers when they're alone with their thoughts.**

These colleges understand that age is just a number. It's part of who we are, of course, but it's not the whole picture. Our age doesn't have to define us. Start thinking of age as a general guideline created by writers when they're alone with their thoughts. Remember that a great deal can happen—and many changes can be made—between the moment the writer puts that idea down on paper and the moment the director starts shooting the final version of the script on set. Many additional variables are introduced in the interim. When actors' performances are strong, our choices unique, and our preparation thorough, our age becomes less and less relevant to those in a position to hire us.

Similarly, I've seen actors disqualify themselves on the basis of physical type—most often their height. Like our age ranges, the height, weight, body type, and other physical characteristics of the roles we seek to play are imagined by writers in the very early stages of crafting their scripts. Many writers will admit that these choices are often rather arbitrary. As projects come together and begin to take shape, various elements once thought crucial to the storyline can be rewritten and reconsidered. Age and physical type—including height, weight, gender, skin color, and ethnicity—can be counted among those variable elements.

Let me relate a personal story. I'm on the shorter side—shorter than most men I meet—but have booked TV and film roles specifically written for tall, physically imposing characters. One role, in fact, called for an actor 6'6" (or taller) so that he could tower over (and intimidate) two other characters, each played by actors who were 6'2" tall.

Fortunately, I was able to find another way within the context of the script to give the producers what they were looking for—and they were flexible enough to consider a different physical type for their character. I sometimes look back and wonder, though, how many actors may have told their agents, "I'm going to pass on this one. I'm only 6'4" and they're really looking for a giant." My attitude is this: Unless your script calls for me to dunk a basketball, I refuse to be limited by something as arbitrary—and out of my control—as my height.

Remember, it's just as easy to talk yourself into an opportunity—and a role—as it is to talk yourself out of one. Dr. Wayne Dyer called this "rewriting your agreement with reality." Don't

---

Unless your script calls for me to dunk a basketball, I refuse to be limited by something as arbitrary—and out of my control—as my height.

Remember, it's just as easy to talk yourself into an opportunity—and a role—as it is to talk yourself out of one.
---

disqualify yourself on the basis of a detail that can be easily changed. You may be exactly what they're looking for; they may just not know it until you knock their socks off with a strong, memorable audition.

> "When Rosalind Hicks, Agatha Christie's daughter, first saw me, she said, 'That's not Poirot.' I said, 'It is now, my dear.'"
> PETER USTINOV

12. Take a Stage Combat Class

"Well, for me, the real excitement of doing physical things in films, whether you're talking about a fight scene or a stunt sequence or even a love scene, for that matter, is, by necessity, it has to be choreographed very much like a dance. That being said, you have to rehearse it over and over again and find a mathematical precision."

BENJAMIN BRATT

Take a stage combat class. You don't have to go too deep. You don't need to become a stunt performer. But a basic intro class will be helpful throughout your career. It's extremely valuable for reinforcing the back and forth, give and take relationship between scene partners. Except instead of using words, the actors use movements. In this respect, stage combat is actually very similar to dance training.

I once worked in a stage play with a young lady who was very talented—but very inexperienced. Our scene called for her character to storm off stage and my character to grab her by the arm and stop her. In our first rehearsal together, she started charging off stage full force and full speed. Our scene quickly turned into a real-life tug-of-war. She became angry with me and shouted, "You've got to really stop me!" I explained, "No, you've got to understand that this is pretend."

There are practical considerations, as well. We use stage combat techniques to protect our scene partners (and ourselves) and make sure that the blocking is consistent in every take. This is vitally important for our directors, ensuring that we complete the action in the same location every time. We call that "hitting your mark." That's why they put tape on the floor to "mark" your position in television, film, and theater.

On another project, a script called for me to slap a female costar across the face. To my surprise, she asked me to really slap her! She explained that would help her "feel it" and react accordingly. I politely declined. If the scene called for me to stab her, would she expect me to use a sharp knife—instead of a prop knife with a retractable blade? Probably not a good idea … but she would definitely "feel it."

Nobody cares how the actor feels. What's important is how we make the audience feel.

I was surprised at the attitudes and behaviors of these two (very talented) actors. In truth, actors don't have to really "feel it." Nobody cares how the actor feels. What's important is how we make the audience feel. Actors must learn to communicate our characters' experiences on the page realistically for the benefit of our audiences. Three-time Academy Award winner Ingrid Bergman summed it up best: "It's not whether you really cry. It's whether the audience thinks you are crying."

I had a teacher once who used to say that actors are paid experiencers. I disagree. Actors are paid communicators. Take a stage combat class and always be extra careful with scripts that call for physical altercations. In the long run, you'll learn to create performances that are far more convincing for your audiences. More importantly, you'll protect your scene partners and yourself.

> **"It doesn't matter a damn what the actor does or does not feel. It's what the lady down there in the blue hat is feeling."**
> GEORGE C. SCOTT

13. Ask Them to Show You

"Life will teach you, but you have to live long enough to get those lessons."
Cary Elwes

Be careful on set. Be aware that it's very easy ... much too easy ... to injure yourself when doing a stunt—unless you're an experienced, trained, and accomplished stunt person. By the way, even experienced stunt performers make mistakes. I've known a lot of stunt people, and every one of them has some type of nagging injury from a perfectly choreographed stunt that somehow went wrong.

Don't fall into the trap of trying to do your own stunts when you're hired as an actor. Most actors want to please others and feel so grateful to have booked a job that they wish to show their gratitude (and positive, cooperative nature) by offering to do their own stunts. This is a monumental mistake.

Oftentimes, productions will try to cut corners and trim their budgets. They may try to take advantage by asking an actor to perform a stunt on set. In most cases, they should hire an experienced stunt person to double the actor instead.

If you're booked as an actor, and the production asks you to do a physical action you're not comfortable with, here's an effective solution: Ask them to show you how to do it. Ask them to demonstrate the action they're expecting you to perform. (You

Ask them to demonstrate the action they're expecting you to perform.

may have to use your acting skills to pretend that you don't fully understand their request.)

In fairness, some producers may actually be making an honest mistake. They may not understand that the action they're asking you to take could be dangerous and should only be performed by an experienced stunt person. In this case, asking them to show you can help them recognize how feasible the physical action really is—or isn't. There's a financial consideration, as well. This is known as a "stunt bump," or an additional payment they must pay the actor for performing a stunt or physical action in the scene.

Additionally, be very wary—especially wary—of performing any stunt or physical action on the last day of shooting when booked on a good-sized role (for multiple days). In some cases, productions will schedule a potentially difficult or questionable stunt on the actor's last day of shooting. This way, if something goes wrong, the actor has already completed the major part of his or her work on camera.

Burt Reynolds, one of the top box office stars of the 1970s and 1980s, was sidelined for more than a year when a fight scene went wrong in the 1984 movie *City Heat*. He was working with an experienced stuntman who he knew well and had worked with on many other films. The stuntman threw a punch a little too hard and connected. Burt Reynolds' jaw was knocked out of alignment and he developed TMJ, an extremely painful joint disorder.

He wasn't able to chew his food and lost a great deal of weight. Mr. Reynolds appeared at several events looking tired, weak, and sickly—leading many to speculate that he had contracted the AIDS virus. (Rock Hudson had recently announced he had contracted AIDS and raised public awareness to the deadly disease.)

To put people's fears to rest, Mr. Reynolds announced that he was actually suffering from TMJ—because of a fight scene that went haywire. Burt Reynolds, by the way, was a fantastic athlete and a tough-as-nails ex-college football player. If this could happen to one of the leading box office stars in the world—an athlete in top physical condition—it could surely happen to you and me. I wonder how many movies he had to turn down, and how many millions he lost, because of that one bad day on set.

Protect yourself when booked on an acting role. Stay safe on set. Actors are notorious people pleasers. We always want to say "Yes!" Always remember the big picture. You're interested in building and maintaining a long-term career in this industry. In order to do that, you've got to keep yourself in one piece.

> **"An actor would be foolish to do something that might hold up the picture, or more importantly incapacitate him. If an actor does do a stunt he needs to make sure a stunt man stands by to see that it's done correctly."**
> **GLENN FORD**

14. Keep Your Shirt On

> "Your naked body should only belong to those who fall in love with your naked soul."
> CHARLIE CHAPLIN

Keep your shirt on—and all your other clothes too. Don't do nudity. This is a temptation for many actors, particularly young females, early in their careers. In general, these will be smaller roles in larger projects. They may seem like once-in-a-lifetime opportunities, but usually are not.

A student of mine was offered a topless role in a big budget film opposite a major A-lister (who would be fully clothed). She had never done nudity before, and this was far outside her comfort zone. She was seriously considering it, though, because of the opportunity to act alongside a star she had admired for many years. Her agent wanted her to take the part. I didn't.

We discussed this at length and decided it was best for her to turn down this project. I was very happy when she did. Here were the best reasons to say "No" to this role:

1. It would most likely not lead anywhere. It was a tiny role to begin with, and the nudity was gratuitous, at best. It did not seem like an opportunity that would advance her career. Yes, there are no small parts (Secret 8), but that doesn't mean the whole world needs to see you running around in your birthday suit.

2. She would probably have an extremely uncomfortable experience on set. She's absolutely gorgeous, and I imagined that the crew would be leering, gawking, and making inappropriate comments all day. Somebody on set would figure out how to take still photos or cell phone video of her when nobody was watching. I was concerned about her privacy, and the long-term effects of this one-day experience on her mental and emotional well-being.

3. My student is a solid commercial actor. She has booked many commercials and will likely book many more. If the commercial advertisers learned about her topless scene—and they surely would—it could end her commercial career pretty quickly. Commercials are all about the product. The product is the star of the show. Advertising agencies and their well-paying clients don't want anything to reflect negatively on their products and campaigns.

4. Most importantly, there is an army of women who specialize in nude and topless roles (Secret 15: Don't Take the Bait). Their resumes consist entirely of this type of work—and they are very comfortable with it. Why would the film producers even offer this role to someone who had never disrobed on camera before? This was the part that truly made no sense to me. Why not hire an actor who had done many topless roles in the past—and would have no moral apprehensiveness about it? There would be far less risk. There would be less chance of a last-minute change of heart and cancellation that would slow down production.

My advice to actors is not to do nudity early in your career—even if you're in terrific shape and very comfortable with your body. Those images can come back to haunt you in ways that you never could have predicted. They can limit you from future opportunities. Make the decision not to show any skin—at least until you become an established name or acquire a few substantial credits. At that point, you'll have solid representation on your team to properly advise you. You'll then be in a far better position to make this important decision on your own terms.

For the record, you also don't need nude headshot photos or demo reel footage. You never need to disrobe in an acting class—or a photo session. If a teacher or photographer asks you to take your clothes off—or engage in any other inappropriate activity—it's a huge red flag. Run, don't walk when you encounter bottom-feeders like this. They have no place in our industry.

My point here is not to be prudish or tell you how to live your life. It's your body and your life. However, taking your clothes off *on camera* can limit your opportunities in the long-term. It can take you out of consideration for more substantive roles later in your career. Your images will be all over the Internet, as well.

> **"Just the fact that somebody can be sexually exploited and violated, and the first thought that crosses somebody's mind is to make a profit from it. It's so beyond me. I just can't imagine being that detached from humanity. I can't imagine being that thoughtless and careless and so empty inside."**
> JENNIFER LAWRENCE

15. Don't Take the Bait

> "If we don't want temptation to follow us, we shouldn't act as if we are interested. No one ever fell over a precipice who never went near one."
> RICHARD L. EVANS

Think of this one as a cautionary tale. Please don't let this happen to you.

Many years ago, I knew a beautiful young lady—a talented actor and singer from a good family in a small town—who lost her direction very soon after landing in Hollywood. She once explained to me how it all started.

She was a little irresponsible with her finances and found herself falling behind on her rent each month. It really stressed her out. A young lady she knew from the gym told her how she makes quick cash in a pinch—topless and nude modeling. Nobody will ever see those pictures anyway, right?

She made the connection for my friend, who went down to the photographer's studio, shot some racy pictures for a couple of hours ... and then received five hundred dollars in cash at the end of the session.

Bingo. That's how they hooked her. That's how they get attractive young women and men to take pictures that destroy their careers before they even have a chance to really get started. They hook them with the promise of fast cash so they can pay their overdue bills. Those pictures were just the start of a very slippery slope for this young lady. She was next enticed into shooting nude videos and soft-core porn. These were not-so-great movies with lots of nudity that aired late at night on premium cable channels.

Decades later, unfortunately, my friend's entire career has consisted solely of this type of work. You can't do that kind of work for years on end without it affecting you physically, mentally, and emotionally. She's not even a good actor anymore. Anytime she had an opportunity to read for something more legitimate, her performance was way over-the-top and always included a sexual innuendo, even when it wasn't indicated in the script.

We lost touch when she started getting into some even darker stuff. I sometimes wonder, though, what she could have done with her life if she hadn't taken that first set of pictures. She may not have gone down the wrong path if she hadn't taken that first step in the wrong direction. It would have been much better for her to take a second job at odd hours—like a customer service position on the overnight shift, or a weekend gig doing birthday parties for little kids in a princess costume. The artist and poet William Blake said it best: "Better to shun the bait than struggle in the snare."

Disastrous outcomes don't just happen all at once. They're the result of a single misstep and a series of bad choices that just get progressively worse. I remember an old interview with Ben Affleck after he first hit it big in Hollywood. He said that he reminds himself every day before leaving the house that he's one bad decision away from becoming an *E! True Hollywood Story*.

Don't let this happen to you. There are so many distractions and temptations in Hollywood that can take promising actors far, far off-course. My ex-friend became addicted to fast cash and soft porn, but smoking, gambling, alcohol, prescription meds, street drugs, and junk food can hook a person just as easily.

While we're at it, let's start to become hyperaware of other self-defeating thoughts and behaviors that can take us further and further from our most important goals. Perfectionism, pessimism, self-pity, resentment, comparing ourselves with others, one-upmanship, social withdrawal and isolation, procrastination, overspending, refusing help from loved ones, reckless driving, and road rage are just a few examples of guaranteed career-killers. You can probably think of several more. These self-defeating actions and attitudes can keep us from moving forward in life—and making the most of all the beautiful opportunities swirling around us. The more we can "unhook" from self-sabotaging attitudes and behaviors, the better we will become at focusing on the important work that brought us to Los Angeles in the first place.

Remember the big picture. Remember why you came to Hollywood. It's much more difficult than people think to get back on track once we stumble, lose our way, and start barreling down the wrong path. Keep your wits about you. Keep your antennae up. Let's put our attention—and keep our attention—on maintaining a clear, direct path towards our goals. Don't take that first step in the wrong direction. Don't take the bait.

> "I sure lost my musical direction in Hollywood. My songs were the same conveyer belt mass production, just like most of my movies were."
> ELVIS PRESLEY

16. Don't Become a Groupie

"If you change the rules on what controls you ... you will change the rules on what you can control."
Guy Ritchie

Don't be a groupie. Don't become a professional hanger-on or houseguest. Don't buddy up with a well-known star to try and advance your career.

Many actors arrive in Los Angeles and immediately become star-struck. If they meet a well-known celebrity—or even a family member of a well-known celebrity—they start seeing dollar signs. You'd be surprised how quickly a newcomer to Hollywood can lose all sense of perspective. I've seen it happen dozens of times. This is a fairly common trap and can cloud one's better judgement. In the long term, it can take an actor very far off-course. It can take an actor down some dangerous paths too.

Over the years, I've known talented, up-and-coming actors who became overly friendly with star-name actors—or their brothers and sisters—and then allowed themselves to become completely distracted and pulled further and further away from their goals. If actors are not careful, they can be dragged into a great deal of unnecessary (and destructive) personal drama, as well.

I believe these actors feel that if they can become friendly enough with a star-name actor, they'll somehow become star-name actors themselves by association. They'll create successful careers for themselves by osmosis.

... the celebrity will slowly, carefully, methodically start taking advantage of the friendship ...

Unfortunately, what happens instead is that the celebrity will slowly, carefully, methodically start taking advantage of the friendship, calling upon the Hollywood newcomer to assist with a variety of mundane, day-to-day tasks and chores. Stars will ask newbies to drive them to industry events, drive them to the airport, pick up their prescriptions and dry cleaning, house-sit, and take care of their dogs, cats, birds, rabbits, snakes, tarantulas, and Komodo dragons.

There's nothing wrong with extending ourselves for friends, of course. We've all been there, and it's nice to be gracious and helpful whenever we can. Just make sure you're not using your new friendship as a career strategy. Remember, some Hollywood stars—the ones you want to avoid—are also used to throwing their weight around and having their way.

Maintain good boundaries with all your friends—no matter how many zeroes they have in their bank accounts. Never allow yourself to be manipulated, used, and abused. Don't become a millionaire's unpaid personal assistant.

> "A sign of a celebrity is often that his name is worth more than his services."
> DANIEL J. BOORSTIN

17. Learn to Compartmentalize

"The goal is to keep one area of your life that might not be going well from causing unnecessary disruptions in another area."
KAREN FINERMAN

You didn't come to Los Angeles to be the social director of your circle—or this city. Every person in your life doesn't need to meet every other person in your life. Your gym buddies don't need to meet your church friends. Your roommate doesn't need to meet your scene partner. Your landlord doesn't need to meet your agent.

You shouldn't ask your accountant for fitness advice. You shouldn't ask your mechanic for career advice. You definitely shouldn't ask your agent to help you move! There's a great deal of wisdom in the idea of keeping every person in your life "in their proper lane." I'm a strong believer that people should stay in their lanes—and those lanes do not need to merge.

It can reflect negatively on you when two people you introduce to one another do not connect as you think they would or should. If sparks fly between the two of them, guess who both of them will blame. Right. You.

When I first landed in Hollywood, I started dating a young lady I liked very much. We had plans for the afternoon in Santa Monica, but I also needed to stop by my agent's office in West Hollywood. We both lived in the Valley, so the agent's office was

---
It can reflect negatively on you when two people you introduce to one another do not connect as you think they would or should.
---

on the way. The young lady was also an actor, so I thought it would be a nice gesture to bring her into the office with me—and introduce her around.

Bad idea.

While I wasn't "officially" recommending her to my agent for representation, I thought that … if they met casually … and if she piqued my agents' interest … and if they responded positively … I might be doing a good deed for all of them. There were way too many "ifs" in that bad idea of mine.

I won't go into detail, but to my great surprise—and even greater embarrassment—my lady friend behaved pretty badly. She was loud, obnoxious, and inappropriate. In the few minutes we were there, I received several very stern "raised eyebrows" from the head of the department—which I thoroughly deserved.

Afterwards, I had to do a little damage control. Fortunately, I had an excellent relationship with my primary agent at this office. She never held that one incident against me. We worked together for many years. The young lady and I split very soon after that day. George Washington said it best: "Better to be alone than in bad company."

Any time you introduce two people, you are giving an implicit "thumbs up" or "stamp of approval" to each of them.

I was probably a little naive. In retrospect, there were warning signs with this woman that I failed to recognize. This incident was a rude awakening for me. We all need a wake-up call sometimes. However, as a newcomer to Los Angeles, I definitely did not need to receive my wake-up call inside my agent's office.

Any time you introduce two people, you are giving an implicit "thumbs up" or "stamp of approval" to each of them. When you do that, be aware that you are putting your name and reputation on the line. Be sure you know someone very, very well before you introduce them to a trusted member of your inner circle. The career you save may be your own.

> "I would compartmentalize the industry for the same reason you compartmentalize ships. If you have a leak, the leak doesn't spread and sink the whole vessel."
> JOHN REED

18. Don't Slurp Your Soup

> "I respect the social graces enormously. How to pass the food. Don't yell from one room to another. Don't go through a closed door without a knock. Open the doors for the ladies. All these millions of simple household behaviors make for a better life. We can't live in constant rebellion against our parents—it's just silly. I'm very well mannered. It's not an abstract thing. It's a shared language of expectations."
>
> JACK NICHOLSON

Improve your table manners—and your manners in general. There's an old saying. "Little things don't mean a lot. They mean everything."

Over the years, I've often heard people in our industry complain about the poor table manners they observe in others—particularly at industry events and networking functions. Believe me, people notice these things.

When someone demonstrates sloppy (or crude) table manners—and other types of crude public behavior—it's usually a sign of carelessness and disrespect that carries over into many other areas of life, as well. You never want that carelessness and disrespect to carry over into your work.

Be careful not to fall into this trap. As actors, people are always going to see us as public figures, no matter what our present-day salaries and professional credits may be. At auditions, rehearsals, industry events—and meetings with potential agents and managers, especially—we should keep a close eye on our table manners ... and our manners in general. Remember to be nice to waiters and waitresses too.

The Stoic philosopher Epictetus said we should conduct ourselves in life as at a feast. And by "feast," he meant a wedding or other elegant special occasion—not the buffet at your local all-you-can-eat restaurant.

I had an agent years ago who set up a camera in the waiting room of his office. It was connected to a small monitor on his desk. He liked to observe the actions and demeanor of every person waiting to see him. A good agent will always be interested in watching his clients to see how they interact with others in the real world. He knows their actions are a reflection upon the agency and all the other actors on the roster.

Always be on your best behavior. Conduct yourself like a lady. Conduct yourself like a gentleman. You are a public figure—no matter what your current bank balance says. People are watching you, I promise.

> **"Wisdom is the quality that keeps you from getting into situations where you need it."**
> **DOUG LARSON**

19. Two Ears. One Mouth. Do the Math.

> "Half the world is composed of people who have something to say and can't and the other half who have nothing to say and keep saying it."
> ROBERT FROST

Never miss an opportunity to be quiet. The scientist Blaise Pascal said that all of mankind's troubles stem from our inability to sit quietly in a room. He was right.

When I was a young actor in New York, I met and befriended veteran actor Al Lewis, best known for his role as Grandpa on *The Munsters* and Officer Leo Schnauser on *Car 54, Where Are You?*. Al was a terrific guy, and we became good friends, in spite of a near forty-year age difference. He was smart, gracious, and humble. More importantly, he was incredibly generous in sharing his wealth of knowledge and experience on a broad range of entertainment industry subjects. He was a sharp, savvy businessman and investor too. He became an unofficial mentor to me when I was first getting started as an actor.

We would meet for lunch in Greenwich Village. Al Lewis would hold court at the table, regaling me—and the waitstaff—with tales of the old-time showbiz glory days in New York and Hollywood. He loved to talk, and I loved to listen. I soaked up his war stories, business advice, and golden nuggets of wisdom like a dehydrated sponge.

Those lunchtime conversations helped me develop a broader perspective on showbiz—and life in general. Because I was such a good listener, Al Lewis felt comfortable telling me things he might not have shared with another actor my age.

He once told me about the day *The Munsters* was cancelled. I'm a TV and film history nerd. I'm particularly fond of the off-the-wall television programs of the 1960s—and always wondered why CBS cancelled *The Munsters* after only two seasons. I knew the show had high ratings and was making gazillions in toy merchandising. It also worked beautifully in the wacky, avant-garde television landscape of the 1960s. It fit right in with all those other weird shows that broke the stodgy old rules of the '40s and '50s: *Batman, Bewitched, I Dream of Jeannie, Star Trek, Lost in Space, Land of the Giants, Mr. Ed, My Mother the Car, Get Smart, The Mod Squad,* and of course, *The Addams Family.* I could go on and on, but you get the idea. Those were the beloved shows of my childhood, and I'm probably a little prejudiced—but most of them are still popular in rerun today. Through the years, they're been popular enough to spin off many movie adaptations too. So why didn't *The Munsters* get five or six more years on air?

"There's no why," Al Lewis told me. "In television, they never tell you why. They just tell you, 'Don't show up Monday.'" That show's cancellation was a tremendous disappointment, I'm sure, but I never heard him complain about it. I never saw any bitterness or sarcasm. He never played the blame game. That's the mark of a seasoned pro. Spending time around him—and keeping my mouth shut—helped me become a seasoned pro too.

I learned a lot from my famous friend. But the best lesson I learned was the one I taught myself: to keep quiet. Because I never would have learned a damn thing if I had been yapping non-stop, trying to impress him with my own stories of recent auditions and bookings.

I let Al Lewis talk. In the process, I let myself listen and learn.

Very often, people talk too much out of nervousness and self-consciousness. I've seen actors talk themselves out of jobs many, many times. The best way to calm down a racing mind is by calming down your physical movements. Quieting the body also helps quiet the mind. Quieting down allows you to focus, concentrate, center yourself, breathe deeply, and become more aware of your environment. When you do that, you're better able to see the myriad opportunities swirling all around you each day.

This is not only beneficial when speaking with a friend and mentor like Al Lewis, but is particularly helpful when interviewing with a new agent or meeting a new contact at an industry event. We're born with two ears and one mouth. Use them proportionately. Listen twice as much as you speak. In the long run, you'll have a lot more to say.

> **"If I'm going to learn and grow, I must know what questions to ask and know how to apply the answers to my life. Listening has taught me a lot more than talking."**
> **JOHN C. MAXWELL**

20. Master the Fine Art of Listening

> "What I do for a living is listen."
> **VAL KILMER**

While the previous section deals with listening to reputable people who can help guide you—teachers and mentors—this chapter's focus is slightly different. The focus here is on acting technique. It's the only suggestion I'll offer on technique in this book, but it's the quickest and most reliable way I know to improve your acting skills and castability.

It's important to *listen actively* when performing a scene. Many actors don't pay close enough attention to their scene partners' lines of dialogue. You can often see it on their faces at auditions and in acting classes. They're just sitting back, waiting for their chance to talk. They look like hungry lions waiting to pounce.

But good acting is always a give-and-take, never a take-and-take. An indispensable component of good acting is reacting. Actors must be fully engaged in the action of the scene—whatever that action may be. Actors must learn to listen, absorb, and be fully affected by the words of the other character in the scene. Alan Rickman said it best: "All I want to see from an actor is the intensity and accuracy of their listening."

Always allow yourself the luxury of becoming fully affected by, and immersed in, the efforts of your scene partner. Allow every word they speak to fully sink in and affect you. This is easier to accomplish when you're fortunate enough to be working with

> **Make the other actor in the scene the most important person in the world to you—either positively or negatively. Raise the stakes as high as humanly possible. Then use your creativity to raise the stakes even higher.**

terrific dialogue. My old friend and acting coach Ralph Marrero used to say, "Sometimes, the words alone are enough."

It's much more difficult when the dialogue you're working with is poorly written, stiff, or just plain uninspired. That happens sometimes. In those cases, there's a technique that will usually work. Make the other actor in the scene the most important person in the world to you—either positively or negatively. Raise the stakes as high as humanly possible. Then use your creativity to raise the stakes even higher. Make that other actor the one, true, great love of your life on the day you must say goodbye forever. Alternatively, make your scene partner a lifelong enemy you're secretly plotting to murder. Hang on that other actor's every word. Listen for clues. Honor every beautiful gold nugget of speech, physicalization, and body language they offer. File it all away in your mental rolodex—so you can use it later in the scene. Notice everything. Soak up every drop of their dialogue—and every subtle gesture—and retain it.

One of the things that makes acting a little confusing for newcomers is the variety of ways in which acting teachers explain certain abstract concepts. Actors must be fully present, in the moment, grounded, connected—whatever you wish to call it. These are all just different ways of describing the same thing: total focus and commitment to the role. The most effective way to accomplish this is to give the other actor your one hundred percent undivided attention. Listen, listen, listen. Become the best listener you know. Listen actively. Active listening and being fully engaged with your scene partner will always set you apart from the other actors in your category.

Ernest Hemingway knew a thing or two about writing good dialogue. He spent quite a bit of time here in Hollywood adapting his—and other novelists'—work for the screen. Hemingway's advice was meant for all people, but is particularly useful for actors. "When people talk, listen completely," Hemingway told us. "Most people never listen."

> **"The big secret in acting is listening to people."**
> ELI WALLACH

21. Not Everything Requires Your Response

"Between stimulus and response there is a space. In that space is our power to choose our response. In our response lies our growth and our freedom."
VIKTOR FRANKL

When actors congregate, there's a tendency for the conversation to turn negative or inappropriate. Many actors talk too much. A lot of actors—particularly at auditions and on set—seem to believe that everything someone says or does requires a clever comment or cutesy comeback. Probably because of their sheer number—and the speed with which actors blurt them out—these comments turn overly negative and sarcastic … and often move towards inappropriate sexual innuendo, as well.

I've known actors who could never control their mouths in public. They talk too much. They talk too loud. And they talk at the wrong time. I've learned to diligently avoid them at auditions, callbacks, rehearsals, bookings, parties, and industry events. (See Secret 39: Don't Be Guilty by Association.)

In the process, they talk themselves out of jobs and future opportunities. Their auditions, by the way, are usually horrible. Do you know why? Because instead of concentrating on the script, they're busy planning out their next joke.

Maybe it's nervousness. Maybe it's stress. Maybe it's narcissism. Maybe it's a never-ending need to be the center of attention. It doesn't matter. We all must learn to edit ourselves. The first thing that pops into your head is not necessarily the right thing to say—especially in a professional setting like an audition or a job. Learn to tame your tongue. Learn to focus on the reason you're in the room. Learn to concentrate completely on the task at hand.

Actors don't always need to be talking. We don't always have to be the center of attention. We don't have to fill up every quiet moment with our nervous banter. We don't always have to show the world how smart, funny, and quick-witted we are. Let people figure that out for themselves from our actions—and our auditions. Arrogance requires advertising, but quiet confidence speaks for itself.

Don't fall into the trap of mindless chit-chat. I've never seen it work in an actor's favor. I've never heard a casting director say, "Bring back that guy who was so funny in the waiting room."

Keep the main thing the main thing. Remember why you're auditioning today. You're here to work. You're here to book this job. You're here to build your credits and career. Not everything you see and hear requires your clever commentary. But every person you're talking to—and every script you're working on—requires your full, complete, and diligent attention.

> **"A healthy male adult bore consumes each year one and a half times his own weight in other people's patience."**
> **JOHN UPDIKE**

22. You're Not a Walking Resume

> "I know an awful lot of Hollywood people who are so self-important, I can't understand it."
> MICKEY SPILLANE

Every conversation you have with industry folks does not have to revolve around your credits, resume, head shots, demo reels, and representation. In meetings, as a matter of fact, industry professionals would rather hear something else. They will often invite actors to "Tell me about yourself." For some bizarre reason, most actors fall apart at this request. They shouldn't. I believe actors get thrown in this interview scenario because they think of it as a "gotcha" question. It really isn't.

Actors should have a short but interesting personal story or anecdote to share. Always keep it positive. Most importantly, we should be able to converse intelligently on a few subjects other than show business. When industry professionals ask you to tell them about yourself, they're essentially opening a door for you. That's not a "gotcha." That's a green light and should never intimidate you. Basically, they're letting you know they want to get to know you better as a person—as a real, living, breathing, human being—because they're potentially interested in working with you … and building a mutually beneficial working relationship together for the next decade.

Accept their invitation. Let the real you come shining through. You were a human being long before you became an actor, and

> **You were a human being long before you became an actor, and you should remain a well-rounded human being with interests, skills, and knowledge outside your show business life.**

you should remain a well-rounded human being with interests, skills, and knowledge outside your show business life. "Be yourself," Oscar Wilde told us. "Everyone else is already taken."

Additionally, actors (and artists in general) are forever in danger of becoming too self-involved. Academy Award winner Paul Newman said it best: "You can't stop being a citizen just because you have a Screen Actors' Guild card." Don't be the actor who's always talking about his own pictures, auditions, bookings, and social media presence. People will pay attention at first, but they will tune you out eventually. Try instead to be an actor who is outwardly focused. Ideally, become a problem solver for others if you possibly can (Secret 34: Think like a Producer).

Put some variety in your life too. Have a rich, full life outside of show biz—or at least a couple of other interests you can converse about intelligently in an agent's office or at a party. It doesn't make you any less of an actor if you have a passion for Italian cooking, horseback riding, animal rescue, shooting billiards, collecting comic books, or practicing origami.

On the contrary, outside activities are healthy, expand your mind, and give you a fresh perspective on life. If you need help with this one, then pick up an adult education catalog and take a class in a subject outside our industry that appeals to you. Who knows? You might even be educating yourself in an area that will be helpful in an upcoming audition or job.

Have a rich, full life outside of show biz —or at least a couple of other interests you can converse about intelligently in an agent's office or at a party.

The smartest, most interesting people I've met understand that all development is self-development. Make your own self-development a lifelong project—and the greatest accomplishment of your career. Start building a better you.

> "I had a friend who worked at a hospice, and he said people in their final moments don't discuss their successes, awards or what books they wrote or what they accomplished. They only talk about their loves and their regrets, and I think that's very telling."
>
> BRAD PITT

23. Use Your Voicemail

"I had never wanted to meet most of the people that I had met, and the fact that I never got to know most of them took dedication and steadfastness on my part."
GORE VIDAL

I think voicemail is the greatest invention of all time. When I look back on the biggest mistakes and worst decisions of my life, they always seem to have been set in motion when I rushed to pick up the phone instead of letting it go straight to voicemail.

I'm not advocating tuning out the world and becoming a hermit. Far from it. But there's something to be said for maintaining your focus and not allowing people to call you at all hours of the day and night—and take you off course and off your game. Don't let friends, family, neighbors, classmates, coworkers, and romantic partners distract you from finishing what you started, keeping your promises, meeting your deadlines, and fulfilling your destiny here on Planet Earth.

This principle is especially relevant to our creative and artistic choices. Director Stanley Kubrick said: "I don't always know what I want, but I always know what I don't want." There's a brilliant strategy here. In the creative process, knowing which ideas we *don't want* to pursue—and sending them to voicemail—helps narrow our focus so that we can get closer to the ideas that will ultimately become the most productive for our careers and long-term growth. (These are the ideas that Mr. Kubrick *did want*.)

You came to Los Angeles for a reason. This is a rough business even for people with unlimited time, money, energy, and resources.

You came to Los Angeles for a reason. This is a rough business even for people with unlimited time, money, energy, and resources. It's even harder to do what you came here to do, unfortunately, when you're spending all your free time driving people to the airport, carrying couches and refrigerators up and down narrow stairwells, and listening to all your unemployed friends complain about how nobody will give them a chance. As you've probably guessed, this is one lesson I definitely learned the hard way.

In my younger days, I wasted a lot of time around people who didn't value my time. Maybe that sounds harsh, but I'd rather you hear it from me than experience it for yourself. Beware of people who will waste your time. They are everywhere in Hollywood.

It's great to have an active social life, but be cautious, canny, and selective about who you allow into your innermost circle. Find friends who lift you up, not pull you down. Stay away from people who put you down, push you around, belittle your hopes, dreams, plans, and ambitions, and are overly negative or sarcastic most of the time. Some people will sink the entire ship simply because they can't be the captain. So be very careful who has your ear—and who you spend time around. Don't be afraid to set strong, definite boundaries. The only people who will

If you're the smartest, hardest working, most ambitious actor in your circle, then it's time to find yourself a new circle.

have a problem with this are people who have no boundaries. Unfortunately, a lot of people you'll meet in Hollywood have no boundaries.

You can waste your life away in Hollywood puttering around with the wrong people. Birds of a feather flock together. You want to fly with eagles, not flop around with chickens. We are the reflection of our five closest friends in life. If you're spending most of your time with five lazy, complaining, surly, uninspired, do-nothing actors, there's a pretty good chance you'll become the sixth. If you're the smartest, hardest working, most ambitious actor in your circle, then it's time to find yourself a new circle. You may have to cut some ties—or at least limit interaction—with people who are holding you back. Voicemail is a terrific tool to help you stay focused and on track while you're making that determination.

> "I recommend limiting one's involvement in other people's lives to a pleasantly scant minimum. This may seem too stoical a position in these madly passionate times, but madly passionate people rarely make good on their madly passionate promises."
> — QUENTIN CRISP

24. Watch Your Language

"I don't like cursing in movies. I feel like cursing has become the new hackiness. You try to find substitutions for cursing."

Zach Galifianakis

Keep it clean. Don't curse. Resist the temptation to use bad language in public. Using foul language gives the appearance of being crude, mean-spirited, and unable (or unwilling) to conduct ourselves like civilized human beings in polite society. When we curse, we might embarrass a potential employer in public. Believe me, movie studios, television networks, and talent agencies don't like to be embarrassed in public.

This is not about being prudish. Rather, this is a practical consideration for how to conduct your business—both personal and professional—in Hollywood. It's surprising, in fact, how many otherwise intelligent people have trouble following this simple, commonsense guideline.

Cursing demonstrates an inability to find more descriptive language with which to express yourself. In the early days of Hollywood, Groucho Marx called this "intellectual laziness." In today's Hollywood, Jay Leno agrees. I spent a good deal of time around Mr. Leno when he was hosting *The Tonight Show*. In eleven years, I never once heard him curse backstage—not even when props weren't working or a VIP guest was running late.

Remember that, in show business, actors are always considered "public figures," no matter what our present-day salaries and credits may be. When we curse, we give the subtle impression that we're not in control of our mouths, our minds, and our emotions. Alternatively, when we react calmly to situations around us that may be going haywire (like well-mannered, well-adjusted adults), we show the world that we're fully in control and capable of handling daily crises as they arise. Jay Leno understands this principle well, and his calmness, professionalism, and strong leadership on the NBC set made everyone around him—cast, crew, staff, executives, and VIP guests—feel safe, confident, and protected.

Cursing is a bad habit and works against our interests when we least expect it. There might be children nearby who can overhear us. We could also offend someone in a position to hire us in the future.

In contrast, using clean language will never work against you. Think about it logically. There is a tremendous potential downside and zero potential upside. Edit yourself. Take out the bad words. There's no discernible benefit to having a sewer mouth in Hollywood.

In all my years in this industry, I've never heard a casting director say: "I don't like that actor. I'm not bringing him in again. He's too squeaky clean. He doesn't curse enough."

> "I was raised to think cursing makes you look unintelligent."
> CHLOE GRACE MORETZ

25. Your Hand Can Shake You Right Out the Door

> "A person who is keen to shake your hand usually has something up his sleeve."
> ALEC GUINNESS

There's a small group of people in Hollywood who are germaphobes. They don't like shaking hands with strangers. They are pretty obsessive about it. They felt this way pre-pandemic, and the years since 2020 certainly haven't made them feel any more comfortable.

Honestly, I can't say I blame them. Los Angeles is the second-largest city in America and also has an international airport. That means people are constantly bringing in bacteria, allergens, and exotic strains of the flu from abroad. Together with the pollution and the normal, day-to-day stress of living and working in this rigorous, highly competitive environment, these combined elements can wreak havoc on our immune systems over time.

Add to this mix all the people who just pumped gas ... and all those who didn't wash their hands after visiting the rest room. I don't want to shake hands with them, and neither does anyone else in the industry.

Casting directors, especially, must be wary about shaking hands with every person they meet, especially during flu season. They may meet and audition fifty to one hundred actors in a day.

Out of nervousness, many actors want to shake hands at auditions and meetings. Besides spreading germs, these actors are also putting casting directors in an awkward situation. Casting directors in live sessions may be juggling the script, the appointment list, the sign in sheet, running the camera, and also watching the clock. That's a lot. Actors who feel compelled to shake hands are slowing them down, inconveniencing them, and making their jobs slightly more difficult. They're putting that casting director on the spot. Not very smart.

> **It's never a good idea to put people who can hire us in an awkward, uncomfortable position.**

It's never a good idea to put people who can hire us in an awkward, uncomfortable position. Do yourself a big, big favor. Let go of this old-fashioned idea that you have to shake hands with everyone you meet in a business setting. Yes, shake their hands if they offer them first, of course. Always be polite and gracious when they do that. But never put anyone in the entertainment industry on the spot by initiating a handshake yourself.

> "I dread handshakes. I've got some problems with my hands, and everywhere I go, people want to impress me with their grip. To make it worse, now women are coming up with that firm shake. So I'll say, 'Gimme five!'"
> GEORGE FOREMAN

26. Don't Stink Up the Room

"I grew up in the East Village with a lot of old people in my building, and I'm not sure if they lost their sense of smell over the years, but they always seemed to smell like they poured a bottle of perfume on themselves. I never want to become that person."
SARAH HYLAND

Go easy on that spritzer, ladies and gentlemen. Better yet, don't wear any perfume or cologne at all. Some folks in our industry are extremely sensitive—and even allergic—to perfumes and colognes. And many people who use it nowadays … use way too much of it.

I knew an actor whose talent agent was well-known for her extreme sensitivity to smells. This agent was so highly allergic, she might stop breathing and have to go to the emergency room if exposed to too powerful a scent. There was a sign posted prominently on the office door requesting that anyone wearing perfume or cologne return on another day—when they're not wearing any. However, please DO NOT ENTER today.

This is an extreme example, of course, but you're far better off going out on a business appointment "au natural." Besides, your perfume or cologne might remind an agent or casting director of another person who wore the same fragrance … maybe another person who was not their favorite person!

None of this is worth the risk. Play it safe. Play it smart. Play it professionally. There's too much potential downside and zero potential upside. Save your fancy perfume and cologne for a hot date. Never wear it on a business appointment in Hollywood.

My friend's agent, by the way, was a gracious, kind-hearted person who was well-known in the industry for going the extra mile for her actors. She had an open-door policy with the actors on her roster and kept a spare room in her office stocked with groceries. Her actors knew that if they ever fell on hard times, they could stop by the office and pick up a bag of groceries for the week. She didn't want her people to skip a meal when times were tough. She didn't want them to have to choose between paying the rent and buying food.

How many business owners do you know who would think of doing that for their clients? Can you imagine actors repaying her kindness by sending her to the emergency room—because they were thoughtless enough to barge into her office dripping with strong perfume or cologne? When we meet generous, well-intentioned people in our industry, let's be sure to respect their boundaries one hundred percent—even if it makes things a little inconvenient for us from time to time.

> **"I don't wear a lot of perfumey-perfumes because I think a lot of them smell like you're wearing perfume. And I don't want to smell like that."**
> **ZOE KRAVITZ**

27. Pay Attention. Eyes Open. Head on a Swivel.

"To be an artist means never to avert one's eyes."
AKIRA KUROSAWA

Understand your environment. Get a clue. Don't be oblivious. The novelist Henry James said it best: "Try to be one of those on whom nothing is lost."

Police officers use the term "situational awareness" to describe their ability to become hyperaware of their surrounding environment. This is a sixth sense or intuition they develop. It tips them off when something in their immediate environment is not quite right … and may signal impending danger.

Actors need to develop situational awareness, as well. Get in the habit of scoping out your immediate environment. Start analyzing it and the people around you. There is a practical benefit to this strategy for walking through the world.

Developing hyperawareness will stop you from saying or doing the wrong thing at the wrong time in the wrong situation with the wrong person. It's vitally important to notice when people are stressed, having a bad day, or simply not interested in what we have to offer. You never want to compound someone's stress level by passing them your card—or hitting them up for an audition or job—when they're busy, distracted, or overwhelmed. Knowing how to walk away shows intelligence, maturity, and class. You

> **People remember us in life for the problems we solve or the problems we create.**

may meet that person on another day when the situation is better. They may remember your instincts and good sense. They may remember the good judgement you showed in your prior encounter. People remember us in life for the problems we solve or the problems we create.

As a minor example, I can't even tell you how many times I've seen groups of people congregating in doorways, chatting away amongst themselves, completely oblivious to their environment—and preventing other people from entering or exiting the room. You don't ever want to be that person at an important meeting or industry event. This all comes down to situational awareness.

Think about it. Developing hyperawareness of their environment is a process that helps keep police officers alive. It's a skill actors should develop too. It will help you in show business—and every business.

Train yourself to become an active, highly attentive observer of everything going on around you. Start noticing every minute detail. Challenge yourself to become more curious about the world and everyone in it. Become a student of human nature, human behavior, and human psychology. In addition to keeping you safe, the skill set you develop will give you important clues on how to incorporate the actions and physicalization you observe

---
Train yourself to become an active, highly attentive observer of everything going on around you.
---

into every character you play on stage and screen. Studying all these things diligently will make you a better actor in the long run.

> "I was always an observer, even as a child. I could be satisfied to sit in a car for three hours and just look at the street go by while my mother went shopping."
>
> JONATHAN WINTERS

28. Beware the Green-Eyed Monster

> "Compare yourself to who you were yesterday, not to who someone else is today."
> **Jordan Peterson**

You will meet a lot of actors in Hollywood. You'll meet some of the best actors in the world ... and some of the worst. Once in a while, some will land major roles—the kind that bring them terrific visibility, colossal paychecks ... and sometimes both.

There's a tendency in this town to put down, belittle, and denigrate those major accomplishments. This is especially true among actors of a similar physical type to us—those we consider "the competition." This is probably a deeply ingrained, highly competitive aspect of human nature. Nevertheless, I believe this is exactly the wrong approach if you're looking for long-term success and staying power in Hollywood.

It doesn't diminish you to praise and to congratulate another actor—even one who resembles you physically. Someone else's success doesn't take anything away from you. I've never believed there's a finite number of acting jobs out there in the world. When someone else books a beaucoup role, it doesn't mean there are none left for you and me.

An early acting teacher of mine, Ralph Marrero, really drilled this in to us. Ralph often said that it doesn't take anything away from us to acknowledge another actor's skill set and accomplishments. He was absolutely right. Neuroscientist Dr. Joe Dispenza describes this in more practical terms. "You are never deprived when someone else gains," Dr. Dispenza explains, "because abundance expands proportionately to match desire."

Be humble, gracious, and grateful. The ability to congratulate your fellow actors, celebrate their victories, and recognize their accomplishments (out loud) will always make you stand out in a crowd. It shows people you're a class act. This is especially true with your close friends and romantic partners. You should be able to congratulate them, wish them well enthusiastically—and really mean it! And you should be able to do all these things without asking, "When is my turn coming?" Aristotle explained this principle beautifully two thousand years ago: "The best friend is he that, when he wishes a person's good, wishes it for that person's own sake."

Jealousy is the most useless—and probably the most destructive—of all human emotions. It is a complete waste of your time, talent, energy, mental focus, and life force. Jealousy is always outer-directed. It drains you and distracts you from focusing inwardly on the things that are most important and can truly help you get to the next level in your career.

Focus on yourself, never on others. Over the years, I've seen dozens of talented actors get completely swallowed up and consumed by their own jealousy over not getting an audition, a role, an opportunity, or an agent. It was like a black hole of chaos and destruction that they allowed themselves to fall into—and oftentimes eagerly embraced. Most of these actors are not even in the industry any longer. They couldn't stand watching other people's careers grow while their own careers remained stagnant—or went downhill. John Wayne challenged this attitude head-on, declaring: "You can't whine and bellyache because somebody else got a good break and you didn't." Don't waste your time, talent, and energy being jealous.

The Roman philosopher Pliny the Elder shared a deeper—and more disturbing—thought on this subject. "Envy always implies conscious inferiority wherever it resides," he wrote. If jealousy has been a recurring issue in our lives, it's probably worth our while to take a deep dive into those thoughts and feelings. Jealousy may be an indication that we're not feeling worthy enough or qualified enough to compete for legitimate roles here in Hollywood. Where did those ideas come from? Who put them in your head? Don't be afraid of a little honest introspection. "The cave you fear," Joseph Campbell taught us, "holds the treasure you seek."

The Green-Eyed Monster is never our friend; it always works against our best interests in subtle, malicious, and manipulative ways. Make a lifelong commitment to be bigger than jealousy. Be above it all. Be happy for all your friends' successes—and help them celebrate. Don't worry if this doesn't come easily to you at first. This is a highly specific skill and requires focus and attention. It's a muscle we build through action, not contemplation. Believe me, this is a muscle well worth developing in Hollywood.

> **"I had a hard time treating my field as if it's horse racing, putting actors in competition against each other. I see how the industry and the studios feel it's important, but I don't really have a feeling for being in competition. I want to feel sympathetic and close to others, not opposed to them."**
>
> **ALAN ARKIN**

29. Be Flexible. Be Adaptable. Be Bookable.

"I was smart enough to go through any door that opened."
Joan Rivers

Many actors say, "I just want to work."

Okay. Great. Where? In which area of our business? Television, film, stage, commercials, hosting, improv, voice-over, print, stunts? In which area of the biz do you feel most comfortable working? Which area is your personal favorite? In which area are you most skilled? In which area do you book most frequently?

Believe it or not, the answers to these questions are often not the same. You may need to train yourself to be more versatile on stage and screen—and develop several different styles of acting to accommodate the many and various opportunities that will present themselves throughout your long career. More importantly, you need to train yourself to be adaptable and ready to move forward when an opportunity presents itself from an unexpected direction.

Jean Carol, an accomplished actor and dear friend—and one of the nicest ladies I've ever met—has enjoyed a career that illustrates this point perfectly. I've known Jean for many years. She is absolutely hilarious—a laugh riot. Jean has a great sense of humor, rapid-fire comedic timing, and is a terrific improvisor.

We called her "a sitcom waiting to happen." Interestingly, she achieved massive success in a very different area—soap operas. Jean is best known for her Emmy-nominated role as Nadine Cooper on the CBS daytime drama *Guiding Light*. Jean has been successful in many other areas of the business, as well, but her breakout role on *Guiding Light* was a pivotal early opportunity for her. She ran with that opportunity and was smart enough to make the most of it.

Guiding Light made Jean Carol a television star and a household name. I know she would have done equally well on a sitcom—and would have made the most of that opportunity if it had presented itself first. As fate would have it, that wasn't the door that opened for her.

I believe the lesson to be learned from Jean's example is to remain openminded about all your audition opportunities. I've known many strong actors who refused to audition for commercials, for example. This is a mistake. One of those actors could become the next Flo from the Progressive Insurance campaign.

You may also remember iconic commercial characters like Josephine the Plumber, Mr. Whipple, and the Maytag Repairman. Stop and think about those actors for a moment. Do you think the performers who played those roles—and cashed those mammoth paychecks—ever imagined these would be their breakthrough roles on television? Do you think those particular actors anticipated those particular opportunities when they took their first acting classes, scheduled their first headshot sessions, and typed up their first resumes? I seriously doubt it. But one thing is certain: none of those actors ever told their agents, "I want to be a serious thespian. Please don't send me out for commercials."

Commercials airing in Los Angeles can give you tremendous visibility to help you get booked on episodic TV and film.

Having a commercial on air, by the way, is a fantastic tool to help you be seen for television and film. Your agent can use the commercial to help pitch you for an unrelated project. "You gotta see my guy for the *Godzilla* movie. He's the young guy sharpening pencils in the *Office Depot* commercial." "Oh, yeah. I've seen that guy. He's great. I love that spot. Let's bring him in." Get the picture? Commercials airing in Los Angeles can give you tremendous visibility to help you get booked on episodic TV and film.

Remember, the way we see ourselves is not necessarily the way the industry is going to see us. Be flexible. Be ready to adapt to every opportunity that comes your way in show business. Opportunity is a quick-change artist and a master of disguise. The opportunities that find us are often very different opportunities than the ones we go looking for.

> "I think every American actor wants to be a movie star. But I never wanted to do stupid movies. I wanted to do films. I vowed I would never do a commercial or a soap opera—both of which I did as soon as I left the Acting Company and was starving."
>
> **KEVIN KLINE**

30. Theater Credits Count

"Do some work in the theater, if you can. It is the best training you can get."
JULIET MILLS

There's a long-standing myth that Los Angeles is a "television and film town" … and nobody here cares about your theater credits and training.

Wrong.

While it's fair to say that New York and Chicago are generally considered "theatre towns," Hollywood agents and casting directors definitely recognize and appreciate the value of solid theater training and credits.

Theater work is always time-intensive. Stage actors frequently spend six nights a week in rehearsal—all the way up until opening night. The best stage actors are trained to be good team players, exactly the type of people you want to collaborate with on long-term film, television, and hosting projects.

A long list of theater credits on an actor's resume tells industry folks you're a team player, work well with others, and have the focus, discipline, and tenacity to make it through the long rehearsal process—all the way up until opening night. It also demonstrates your ability to book a job, show up on time every day, memorize your lines, take direction, and not get fired for doing something stupid.

There are dozens of small theaters in Los Angeles and the surrounding area. If you're really having trouble finding an agent, landing auditions, and booking television and film work—then roll up your sleeves and start working on stage. I believe there's no better training ground for learning your craft. Shirley Knight said it best: "My goal was not to be famous or rich but to be good at what I did. And that required going to New York and studying and working in the theater."

The good news is that you don't have to go to New York or Chicago to work in the theater. You can realistically perform in four to six new stage plays per year right here in Los Angeles—and even more if you really hustle. Before you know it, you'll build up a solid resume of theater credits. You'll get practical working experience—the kind of experience that is invaluable to actors. You'll learn so many things that are far beyond the scope of what you can learn in an acting class. You'll learn stagecraft, voice control and modulation, comedic timing, and how to think quickly on your feet. You'll figure out what to do when props don't work and scene partners miss their cue. You'll master the art of getting the storyline back on track when another cast member skips an important line of dialogue. You'll network with other actors. When their agents come to see the show, they'll also see you.

You'll network with other actors. When their agents come to see the show, they'll also see you.

> **This will make you a much more attractive prospect to all those agents who rejected you when you approach them again in a year or two.**

All these things will benefit you tremendously in the long run. They'll turn you into an experienced, versatile, and resourceful theater actor with a long list of Los Angeles stage credits. This will make you a much more attractive prospect to all those agents who rejected you when you approach them again in a year or two. Remember, your career is a marathon, not a sprint. If you're trying to build your film and TV credits—and really aren't making much progress—then working in the theater can be a terrific indirect route to help you get there.

> "You have to go around the corner
> to get around the block."
> RALPH MARRERO

31. Overcome Skepticism with Specificity

"I encourage active skepticism—when people are being skeptical because they're trying to identify the best course of action. They're trying to identify the next step for themselves or other people."
TIM FERRISS

Because many in Hollywood embellish their credits, training, background, and contacts, it's often difficult to establish trust when meeting someone new. People can be extremely skeptical here.

Ronald Reagan, who was president of the Screen Actors' Guild long before he was president of the United States, had a favorite catchphrase: "Trust but verify." This is a terrific rule for actors. Make it easy for people to verify what you tell them. Specificity will always help you build trust and establish credibility with people you've just met.

For example, if you have a well-known TV show listed on your resume, always include the episode number(s). This way, directors can look up the show and verify your appearance on that specific episode. They can also see who directed your episode and can contact that person—or any other crew member—if they'd like to check up on you a bit. And believe me, people in this industry will check up on you a bit.

Another idea that works well is to include a still photo from a role you've performed as the primary photo on your business card. A picture from a job you've booked will help you overcome any initial skepticism from someone you're meeting for the first time. Most actors use their headshot photo, but a picture of yourself from a working set gives you instant credibility. This can be quirky and memorable—like a photo from backstage, your wardrobe fitting, or the makeup chair. Of course, it's important to make sure you're not violating terms of a non-disclosure agreement (NDA) you've signed. If the job is from a television show, you should wait until your episode has already aired.

People are skeptical in Hollywood—and will absolutely check up on you. Therefore, you also must be careful not to stretch the truth. It's an unfortunate fact that many people who touch down here embellish their resumes, backgrounds, connections, and accomplishments.

The padded resume may not have been invented in Hollywood, but it was certainly perfected here. Aspiring actors have been guilty of lying on their resumes since the early days of silent film. None of them fooled William Wellman back then, and none of them will fool Quentin Tarantino today.

You may be able to pull the wool over the eyes of a beginner, but anyone who really knows what they're doing in Hollywood will see through a lie in ten seconds flat. Never again will they take you seriously. You might be tolerated for a while, but you will never be taken seriously or respected as an equal. "A liar will not be believed," Aesop warned, "even when he speaks the truth."

Don't lie about your background, credits, training, connections, or accomplishments. Most importantly, don't lie about a special skill you don't actually have. Don't put it on your resume if you can't do it expertly today.

As long as you're telling the truth on your resume, in the audition room, and in the Zoom room—and can verify it—you will continue building credibility with people who can hire you in the future.

Until you establish a name for yourself, however, industry folk are going to be a little skeptical of everything you tell them. This is because of all those who have come before you—and who have been less than honest, forthright, and ethical. This is not your fault. However, it's still your responsibility to prove yourself over and over again when you meet new industry contacts. Every time you do, you'll begin to establish a little bit more trust and credibility. Prove yourself enough times, and eventually people will begin to see and expect the very best in you.

Just remember: none of this is personal. It feels personal, but it's not. It's not about you; it's always about them. People who doubt you are trying to protect themselves, their businesses, their careers, and their reputations. This town has seen more than one hundred years of shysters, opportunists, narcissists, plagiarists, and pathological liars come and go. (Many of them, unfortunately, have come and stayed.) Be patient. It may take a little while to convince industry professionals you're not one of them.

The good news is that you can make a conscious decision to behave far more honestly and ethically in your own career. You can be a bright light in an often dark environment. You can build your credits and develop a reputation for hard work, intelligence, creativity, and integrity. That's a great way for you to stand out from all the other actors in your category.

"Tell the truth, but make the truth fascinating."
David Ogilvy

32. Be Mega-Prepared

> "Garbo went through a great deal to get a scene right. She worked out every gesture in advance and learned every syllable of dialogue exactly as written. She never improvised, and I respected her for that."
> — GEORGE CUKOR

Nobody expects you to be perfect. But everyone in Hollywood expects you to be very well-prepared. There is no substitute for diligent, conscientious preparation. Being unprepared for an audition—or worse, a job you've already booked—is pretty much unforgivable here.

Hollywood is full of very strong actors, but even those who are not as skilled often have the art of auditioning down to a science. There are plenty of not-so-great actors who are terrific at auditioning. One of the ways they accomplish this is by being super-prepared for those audition opportunities whenever they arise.

Preparation is the key. Preparation makes good actors better, and it makes great actors extraordinary to watch. Preparation also makes below-average actors castable, meaning that good directors can hire them—and then work with them to get decent performances on set.

Many actors—solid and not-so-solid—also pay private coaches to prep them for important auditions. Fifty to one hundred dollars per hour is the going rate—though several well-known coaches charge far more. Understand that the competition for acting roles

---

… being so well-prepared, and knowing your lines so thoroughly, that it will be impossible to be thrown off your game.

---

is fierce in Hollywood. Most of the other actors reading for your role will be very well-prepared—even those who are not as good as you.

I'm a firm believer in being so well-prepared, and knowing your lines so thoroughly, that it will be impossible to be thrown off your game. Know your lines forward, backward, and sideways. I mean that quite literally—forward, backward, and sideways—so you can pick up a cue seamlessly from anywhere in the script.

Years ago, I booked a supporting role on a new TV show, *Memphis Beat* on TNT. I had two scenes with the series leads, Jason Lee and Sam Hemmings, who were cast as Memphis police detectives in the new program. One of my scenes was very dialogue heavy. I had a lot of lines, including a full-page monologue—which was great. However, the script indicated that my character was going to be handcuffed and interrogated by the two stars. That was a challenge. I knew I wouldn't be able to hide the mini-script anywhere. (In most TV and film roles, the production office will provide a "shrunken down" version of the scenes you're filming that day. It's about four inches by six inches and can easily be stashed away in a pocket when the cameras start rolling.) I knew it would be impossible to refer to my mini-script between takes since I would be handcuffed.

When I showed up on set, I knew that script forward, backward, and sideways. I knew that script better than my own name. I made sure I was so well-practiced with my lines that I could pick up a cue from anywhere on the page effortlessly. That turned out to be a smart choice, because the director made a couple of minor changes in my dialogue—while I was handcuffed. The last-minute changes didn't throw me because I knew all those lines (and the two other characters' lines) so well.

Let me offer a couple of suggestions for memorizing lines. A lot of actors have a lot of trouble in this area. What I like to do when practicing a new scene or monologue is record myself and the other roles (in different voices) in an audio file on my phone. I also like to write out the scenes or monologues on index cards, which I can keep in a shirt pocket—and refer to when I'm not handcuffed. It's also helpful to write out each different character's dialogue in a different color ink.

Some of us are auditory learners. Some of us are visual learners. Some of us are tactile learners. When memorizing lines, it helps to incorporate every different style of learning so that each technique reinforces the others. I like to play the audio recording—while reading through the index cards—and also speaking the lines out loud. That way, I'm seeing the lines visually, while also hearing them, and training the muscles in my mouth to speak them out loud—all at the same time.

Back in the ancient technology era, I recorded audio cassettes of the dialogue (changing my voice for each role) and played them in the car while driving. I would also speak the lines out loud while listening to the tapes on a Walkman (remember those?) whenever I was at the gym or out for a walk with my dog. This is

> **Part of being mega-prepared is offering no excuses. Unprepared actors embarrass themselves and their agents—and drastically limit themselves from future opportunities.**

a technique that has worked extremely well for me through the years. I highly recommend you try it. Incorporating several different learning styles together will work well for newcomers and experienced actors alike.

Keep in mind that most of the other actors reading for your role will absolutely be bringing their A-game into the room with them. Even if they're just average or below-average actors—let's call them C-level actors—being mega-prepared will usually bring them up to B-level when they need to be.

Part of being mega-prepared is offering no excuses. Unprepared actors embarrass themselves and their agents—and drastically limit themselves from future opportunities.

Most actors enjoy the excitement of improv, being spontaneous in the scene, and coming up with new ways to speak their dialogue. Great. Very few actors, though, can handle the tedious and more mundane—even boring—aspects of show business. Be mega-prepared. Go above and beyond. Be super-diligent in learning your lines. It's not terribly exciting while you're writing out those index cards in different color inks—and listening to those audio recordings over and over and over again—but this

Mike Kimmel

Very few actors can handle the tedious and more mundane—even boring—aspects of show business.

---

habit will pay tremendous dividends for you when you book the role and are performing those lines on set.

> "When you're not practicing, someone somewhere is. And when the two of you meet, assuming roughly equal ability, the other person will win."
> BILL BRADLEY

33. Practice Never Makes Perfect

*"We are what we repeatedly do.
Excellence, then, is not an act but a habit."*
WILL DURANT

Aim for progress, not perfection. While it's important to be mega-prepared, understand that practice does not make us perfect. Practice only makes us better. It never makes us perfect. Please give up on the idea of perfection, and accept the fact that you can be one hundred percent castable by being mega-prepared, easy to work with, and dedicated daily to becoming the best possible version of yourself—and the best possible actor.

Even our favorite movie stars have days when they're not at their best. Those days are recorded on camera and remain forever as filmic records of famous, talented performing artists who (usually) gave it their all—but were just a little bit off the mark when the cameras finally started rolling that day.

You might not be at your best on the day of an important audition, but you might still read well enough to book the role. I've seen it happen hundreds of times, and it's happened dozens of times to me personally. Remember Secret Number 1: The Best Actor Doesn't Always Get the Job.

Please understand that I'm not telling you to slack off and be lazy. Far from it. Always be mega-prepared (Secret 32). The talent pool in Los Angeles is gigantic. The competition here is fierce. But even the best actors (and movie stars) have their not-so-great days. You can still book on those days. Don't skip an audition. Don't hide from the world. Don't lock yourself up in your apartment. Don't wait for everything to be perfect. Don't wait for a perfect script. Keep moving forward, even on those days when it feels like you're moving forward at a snail's pace.

During one nice, long stretch, I was on a hot streak and auditioning like crazy. I knew a good booking and payday were right around the corner. Most of the auditions were going well—except for a couple of weird ones with not-so-great scripts.

My agent called with the good news that I booked the *weirdest* of those weird ones. "What?! *That's* the one I booked?! I didn't even understand the script," I told him. "Their script is a piece of garbage," my agent said. "Marlon Brando wouldn't be able to save that script. The casting director said she appreciates that you didn't turn down the audition. A lot of actors did. And every actor who read for her last week was horrible—but she told me you were 'the least horrible guy in the room.'"

I put that on my business card for a while:

Mike Kimmel
SAG-AFTRA
The Least Horrible Guy in the Room
Call for Rates

That movie turned out to be a nightmare. Everything went wrong. Picture the Hindenburg falling out of the sky and crashing into the Titanic as they both went down in flames. The producers ran out of money and never even finished shooting. But before it all fell apart, me and my agent made a decent little payday. That

> **Even when you're not nearly at one hundred percent, you may still perform well enough to stumble your way to success.**

wasn't our first choice, of course—but it was a job, and we did it. We fulfilled our obligations. We don't always get to do high art. We don't always get to work with people who are competent. Sometimes, the job is just a job. Sometimes, you take the role, cash the check, lick your wounds, learn your lessons, and move on to the next one. Wash. Rinse. Repeat.

There will be days when you don't even feel like showing up. I promise you, we all have those days. Show up anyway. If we can acknowledge that the best actor doesn't always get the part (Secret 1), then it stands to reason that you may book the part on a day when you're not at your best—and don't even feel like showing up.

Even when you're not nearly at one hundred percent, you may still perform well enough to stumble your way to success. It's hard to stumble onto anything, though, when you're curled up on the couch and hiding from the world. Don't wait to be at your best—and don't ever wait for a perfect script. You can book an acting job in Hollywood by being the least horrible guy in the room.

> "Success is less about luck and more about practice."
> ROBIN SHARMA

34. Think like a Producer

> "I never met a man who was good at making excuses who was good at anything else."
> BENJAMIN FRANKLIN

We all need to train ourselves to become problem solvers and think like producers—not actors. That means no excuses and no complaining. Try instead to figure out how you can become a problem solver for productions who can hire you. As actors, we're often so focused on our own roles that we don't take time to think about how we fit into the project as a whole.

Producers think much differently. They need to see the big picture so they can identify problems before they arise. A problem is anything that can cause a delay, increase costs, create legal issues, or prevent the project from being completed on time and under budget.

Actors are generally the last ones hired on a project. Producers and directors understand that—once the money is in place, locations are secured, and all the behind-the-scenes creatives have been hired—then they can get to work on casting the actors. The reason is simple. There are more than enough skilled actors for every role. This is true even at the star level. When an A-lister drops out of an upcoming project, it's usually not that difficult to replace him or her with another A-lister.

Don't make excuses and don't complain. Acting is a solo craft. Embrace the solitude. Nobody's coming to the rescue. We all need to take personal responsibility for our careers, finances, peace of mind, and physical, mental, and emotional health here in Hollywood. There's an old Swedish proverb: "The best place to find a helping hand is at the end of your own arm."

Many actors place responsibility for their success squarely on the shoulders of other people in their lives—usually their agents. Talent agents, however, often say that the actors who really pique their interest are those who are the most proactive and consistent in building their credits and developing their careers. A common lament among talent agents, in fact, is that they only earn ten percent of the money—and their clients expect them to do one hundred percent of the work!

Resourcefulness is one of the most valuable traits actors can develop. Resourcefulness is the skill producers use to overcome their own excuses. Day-to-day success in show business is often related to what we can do right when things go wrong. What can you do when you're pressed for time and the money dries up? What can you do while you're working at a full time job? What can you do on your lunch break? What can you do without an agent? What can you do with limited experience and without any contacts?

Producers and directors face these same challenges too. When shooting outdoors, they ask themselves, "What can I do while the sun is still out? What can I do before we lose the light? Can I

Day-to-day success in show business is often related to what we can do right when things go wrong.

---

shoot another scene or B-roll while I'm waiting for a cast member who's running late?" Even on big budget projects, resourcefulness and flexibility always come into play to help get projects completed on time and under budget.

The best actors I've met always seem to be the hardest working—and the best outside-the-box thinkers. Many of them create their own projects and opportunities. They write and produce short films with great roles for themselves and their friends. They create web series, blogs, podcasts, and one-person stage shows. They're always in class. They keep their headshots and resumes up to date. They're active on social media. Most importantly, they don't complain and they don't make excuses.

Every time you point a finger, you have three pointing right back at you. I've always believed that if we all took the time we waste complaining and making excuses—and invested that time in productive activity instead—we'd all be much happier and more successful.

The healthiest way to approach your acting career is with a diligent, long-term focus. The only way we lose is if we quit. I believe actors need to develop entrepreneurial skills to start creating our own work. Our creativity doesn't have to begin and end with the roles we're reading in the scripts strangers have written for us. We can use our own creativity to develop our own projects that show us off at our own very best.

Take a deep dive into this process—and start thinking like a producer from now on. Start strategizing on how to put together your own projects, even if they're on a micro-budget. It's pretty hard to get fired when you're also the producer who put the whole project together. Producers are always problem solvers.

"Expect problems and eat them for breakfast."

They spend most of their time putting out fires and getting all the moving parts to work together as a cohesive whole. The philosopher Alfred Montapert offered us great advice when he said: "Expect problems and eat them for breakfast."

And when we're fortunate enough to be hired as actors on someone else's project, let's keep our eyes on the big picture and the producer's overall goal: Nothing is more important than getting the project completed safely, on time, and under budget. The more you can train yourself to think like a producer, the more valuable you will be to productions that can hire you as an actor.

> "I believed in the concept of over-performing. I believe anyone can achieve their goals in life if they over-perform, and that means you have to work ten times harder than anybody you see."
> STEPHEN J. CANNELL

35. You Should Write Something

> "I think writing really helps you heal yourself. I think if you write long enough, you will be a healthy person. That is, if you write what you need to write, as opposed to what will make money, or what will make fame."
>
> ALICE WALKER

Actors with many years of experience often find themselves getting frustrated with the lack of control they have over their own careers. It's not unusual to hear veteran actors tell one another: "You should write something."

I worked with Vin Diesel back when he was a young, unknown, up-and-coming actor in New York. He's one of the most confident people I've ever met, by the way. I'm sure that confidence had a good deal to do with his success. His first major success, though, came as a direct result of a terrific short film he wrote and starred in titled, *Multi-Facial*. Steven Spielberg saw the film at a festival, loved him in it, and cast him in *Saving Private Ryan*.

Similarly, Nia Vardalos and Chazz Palminteri each found tremendous success with the one-person stage shows they wrote, *My Big Fat Greek Wedding* and *A Bronx Tale*. Both of those plays were later turned into feature films that launched successful careers for their writer-creators. And Mr. Stallone didn't do too badly with that little boxing script he wrote for himself, either.

Try it for yourself. Try putting pen to paper and writing something. The creative writing process is not so very different from the creative acting process. Through examining the backstory of the characters we play, our acting experience gives us unique and practical insights into human psychology. These skills are essential in writing strong scenes and scripts.

Most good actors who try their hands at writing find that they are particularly skilled at writing compelling, realistic dialogue. Story structure takes a little more time, but can still be mastered with practice. Writing great dialogue, though, is a good, solid place to start.

Writing something will also give you a new appreciation for what full-time writers do on a daily basis. You will likely interact with many full-time writers throughout your acting career. It's always helpful to understand their process. A writer is not just a technician who puts words down on the page—any more than actors are technicians who read words off those printed pages.

Write a stage play. It doesn't have to be long. It can be a one-act. Or write a short film with good roles for yourself and your best actor friends that you can produce together on a micro budget. If any of these seem overwhelming to you, then just try writing a single scene that you can perform and tape for your demo reel. If it's not any good, then you haven't lost much time—and you've also gained a little experience.

Writing is a strong creative action step for performers. Put it on your list of things to do. I believe you'll find the process rewarding and enjoyable if you make a solid, serious effort in this area. Doing this will help demystify the writing process for you. Most people are very intimidated by the idea of writing and never know where to start—until they take a deep dive into the process.

Writing gives you a creative outlet that will keep you energized and inspired whenever the auditions slow down. Writing is also an important intermediate step towards directing and producing. If you think you may want to try your hand at directing or producing in the future, writing something now will help you get there.

There's another advantage to writing. You can train yourself to become really good at ad-libbing dialogue when a scene isn't working, when there's a last minute glitch with props or wardrobe, and when a scene partner misses a line or cue. Developing this skill helps you give directors additional options to fix a scene that isn't working well. Some directors, unfortunately, will not be open to this, but the best directors in our industry understand that film is a collaborative process. They are always interested in hearing valuable input, a fresh perspective, and even a few new lines of dialogue from their trusted team members.

> **"I wouldn't have made it this far in my career if I wasn't a great f*cking writer."**
> **JACK NICHOLSON**

36. Get Used to Criticism. You Will Get It.

> "I have pretty thick skin, and I think if you're going to be in this business, if you're going to be an actor or a writer, you better have a thick skin."
>
> JOHN IRVING

Anytime we put ourselves out there in the world as artists, we must get ready for criticism. Some of that criticism will be helpful and legitimate. Some criticism, however, will be completely unwarranted and wildly inappropriate.

It's almost a cliché to hear actors reveal that they never watch their own performances in film and television. Personally, I've never believed those comments. I don't believe any actor who says that.

I've always been a great fan of Jack Nicholson, for example. His performances in major films have been some of the strongest in the last half-century. Look at his early movies, however, and you won't even think you're watching the same actor. I believe Nicholson's early work in Roger Corman's films give no indication of the extraordinary success he would achieve just a few years later.

I would bet my bottom dollar that Jack Nicholson received a ton of criticism for those early, low-budget projects. I imagine he watched those performances with a critical eye and self-corrected —and that's why he became such an extraordinary actor and film legend.

Fred Astaire was criticized early in his career for his receding hairline and the size of his ears. Greta Garbo was criticized for the size of her feet. Marlene Dietrich was criticized for doing a nude scene in a European film before emigrating to the United States. Fred Gwynne was criticized for his height (too tall). Danny DeVito was criticized for his height (too short). Sylvester Stallone was criticized for his thick New York accent.

In showbiz, however, every actor is considered a "public figure"—whether that actor has a star name or not. Criticism for public figures in general—and actors in particular—is often inappropriate, condescending, and mean-spirited. In the Internet age, it's also anonymous.

It's your performance they're criticizing—and not you.

However, actors need to remember this: It's your performance they're criticizing—and not you. Let's tackle criticism with the same tongue-in-cheek attitude Fred Allen did. The old-time host and humorist was a true show biz Renaissance man. Fred Allen hosted popular programs on radio and television, was an inventive stand-up comedian, sang and danced well, played the tuba and ukulele, wrote a column for *Variety*, also wrote several very funny books, and was an expert juggler and ventriloquist. Fred Allen had seen and done it all.

At one point, Fred Allen's stand-up comedy act was criticized so harshly that he commissioned a muralist to paint tombstones on a set of theater curtains that he carried with him on his stand-up comedy bookings. On the tombstones were painted the jokes that bombed most spectacularly for him. The old-time radio, television,

Criticism is deadly, but it only has power over us if we decide to bend our knee to it. That's our choice.

film, and comedy legend also told us: "If criticism had any real power to harm, the skunk would have been extinct by now."

Criticism is here to stay. Get used to it. Get acquainted with it. Make peace with it. Make friends with it. Do whatever internal work you need to do to thicken up your skin. I can promise you that criticism is coming for you—just as it is coming for all of us—and it will be horrific. Be prepared to be criticized in ways you would have never expected or imagined. Criticism is deadly, but it only has power over us if we decide to bend our knee to it. That's our choice. Actors who don't train themselves to handle criticism and rejection are actors who drop out of the business much too soon (Secret 38: The Experts Aren't Always Right).

None of this is fair, but it's all part of the daily price we pay for the opportunity to work, thrive, and advance in this highly competitive industry. Keep pressing forward and prove all your critics wrong. Then prepare yourself to be criticized for something else by someone new—and do it all over again. Wash. Rinse. Repeat. That's how experienced actors train themselves to keep going in Hollywood, no matter what their critics may say.

> "To avoid criticism, do nothing, say nothing, be nothing."
> ELBERT HUBBARD

37. The One-Strike Rule

"No man ever steps in the same river twice, for it's not the same river, and he's not the same man."
HERACLITUS

We've all heard of the three-strike rule. In show business, however, there's less tolerance for breaking the rules—or simply underperforming. It's seldom spoken about openly, but there is a "one-strike rule" in our industry. Agents, casting directors, and producers have learned to protect themselves from under-performers—as well as bottom-feeders, liars, scammers, and con artists—by writing off people they believe will waste their time, cost them money, or damage their reputations. They have learned to be extremely protective of their time, money, and professional credibility.

Early in my career, I was called in to interview with a "Big Three" agency—one of the largest talent agencies not only in New York and Los Angeles but throughout the world. It was a lucky break for me; my photo and resume crossed the desk of a young, up-and-coming agent at the exact time he was submitting for a role that matched my physical description. He secured an audition appointment for me, and asked me to stop by the office before the audition to meet him and get acquainted.

The interview and audition both went well. It would have been a sizable payday if I had booked the part. Unfortunately, I didn't. Actors won't book every job and won't always get a callback, of course. That's not unusual. Most experienced actors understand that this is a numbers game. Though I stayed in touch with this agent for several years afterwards, I never received another call from his office. I was disappointed, of course—but didn't yet understand the one-strike rule.

A couple of years later, a good friend had a similar experience with another powerhouse agency. Like me, my friend did not book his one-and-only audition opportunity from this mega-office. Like me, my friend stayed in touch with the agent. Several years later, he ran into this agent at an industry event and tried to reconnect. My friend is pretty aggressive—sometimes too aggressive—and was bold enough to ask the agent directly why he hadn't been sent out on any more auditions. He was shocked by the gentleman's response. "What are you talking about? I gave you a shot. I sent you out," the agent explained. "You didn't book. Done."

My friend was pretty upset after this exchange, but he made the same mistake I had made years earlier. We were both looking at things from an actor's point of view and didn't yet understand the agent's perspective. To an agent—especially one in a high-powered mega office—time equals money. This is not personal. It's business. Each agency is given a limited number of audition slots by the casting director for every project. An agent who takes a gamble on a new prospect—like me or my friend—is taking an appointment slot away from another actor on their roster who might have booked that job.

It's a complicated issue, and there are no easy answers. I give my friend's agent credit, though, for being so honest and forthright about the way things work from a top-level agency's perspective. Many people in Hollywood prefer to avoid potential

> **An agent who takes a gamble on a new prospect—like me or my friend—is taking an appointment slot away from another actor on their roster who might have booked that job.**

arguments—and would not have been so honest and direct with my friend.

The bottom line is this: with many of the larger agencies and casting offices in Hollywood, you will only get one shot. If you don't book it, get a callback, knock it out of the park, or somehow manage to really capture their attention, they will immediately lose interest and move on to someone else. This is not personal. This is a numbers game from an agent's perspective.

On a side note, I signed with a well-respected mid-sized agency several years later. There were three main agents there and a small army of assistants. I was with them for many years and landed some pretty solid bookings through their office. Coincidentally, we started off on the right foot too, as I happened to book the very first audition they ever sent me out on. Believe it or not, I still didn't understand the full significance of that first job until several years later. That first job wasn't even a big moneymaker, so I never saw it as a game-changer for me or the agency. Again, that's because I was looking at that first booking from an actor's point of view—not an agent's. My agent saw things much differently. It was our very first audition and booking together—and he considered it a good omen of things to come. Apparently, this is an "agent thing."

My agent always remembered that first success together. In fact, he brought it up in conversation with me several times through the years. That first job wasn't a big deal to me, but it was a very big deal to him.

Never lose sight of the fact that this is an incredibly competitive industry. It's often the case that you will only get one shot to make a good impression with a new contact in Hollywood. Many offices, especially the big ones, will never give you a second chance if you don't make money for them on your maiden voyage together.

Things are different for celebrities, of course. We've seen star-name actors have very public meltdowns and deal with personal drama in their private lives out in public for all the world to see. We may wonder why they receive so many second chances. Simple. It's because they've already proven to be bankable commodities. Their names, likenesses, and prior reputations translate to dollars. Even when celebrities' reputations take a hit, smart talent agents can usually figure out how to reactivate their clients' damaged careers. For the rest of us, however, until we show the industry we can bring in gigantic piles of cash—we'll very often only get one shot.

> **"It's not show fun. It's not show play. It's show business."**
> **SCOTT POWERS**

38. The Experts Aren't Always Right

"An expert is a man who has made all the mistakes which can be made in a very narrow field."
NIELS BOHR

I keep a file in a desk drawer of old cast lists and contact sheets from productions I've worked on through the years. From time to time, I go through them and pick up the phone to reconnect with actors I worked with on those long-ago projects. I'm always surprised—and more than a little disappointed—at how many old friends and colleagues have dropped out of the business. The reason is usually the same. Most of them tell me they were in the industry for a long, long time and thought they were pretty good at handling rejection. And then one fateful day, they received particularly harsh criticism from someone whose opinion they valued highly—someone considered an industry expert.

Here's a news flash: The experts aren't always right.

When Charlie Chaplin was the leading box office star in the world, his studio sponsored a Charlie Chaplin look-a-like contest. Dozens of fans showed up decked out in their best Chaplin costumes and make-up. Many of these entrants had been practicing the star's mannerisms and facial expressions for years and were really convincing.

Charlie Chaplin himself decided to show up and enter the contest under a fictitious name. He did this as a joke. As it turned out, the joke was on Charlie Chaplin—because he finished in third place!

That's right. Charlie Chaplin entered a Charlie Chaplin look-a-like contest back in the day—and he came in third. This is one of my favorite old-time Hollywood stories. On the surface, it's a funny anecdote. On a deeper level, I believe it provides a valuable lesson for all performing artists.

Think about the contest judges. More than likely, they were film industry professionals who thought they knew everything there was to know about Charlie Chaplin—the number one box office star in the world—and his career. But they couldn't even recognize the man when he walked through the door that day.

Don't let other people's opinions define you—not even the opinions of experts. Too many good actors let negative comments and poor evaluations from authority figures demolish their self-esteem.

While it's important to accept honest feedback and well-intentioned direction, it's equally important to keep those expert opinions in their proper perspective. Be sure to seek out advice from multiple sources. Not everyone in the industry is going to appreciate our skills and talents. Not everyone is going to "get" us. For every expert, there will be another expert who will disagree. Don't let one bad audition or meeting (or one major career disappointment) make you quit the business. Our sensitivity and vulnerability—the very same qualities that make us good actors—can often wreak havoc in our personal lives.

By the way, think about how bold Mr. Chaplin was on that day. Do you think anyone would really care who won that look-a-like

Mike Kimmel

Don't overthink and overvalue one bad experience or negative evaluation in your career—no matter who it comes from.
---

contest today—or would anyone even know it existed—if Chaplin himself hadn't been creative enough and mischievous enough to sign up and participate? What's keeping you and me from signing up and participating in our own careers to the same degree? What do you think Charlie Chaplin would have said to an industry expert who told him he had no talent and should pack it up and go back home to Merry Olde England?

Learn to get out of your own head and stay out of your own way. We had a clever old saying back in the Bronx: "Stay out of your head. It's a very bad neighborhood." Don't overthink and overvalue one bad experience or negative evaluation in your career—no matter who it comes from.

I wish I could have spoken with some of my old castmates, the actors I worked with years ago, before they made the decision to quit. Most of them were super-talented performers, fantastic team players, and absolutely wonderful human beings. That's why I picked up the phone to reconnect. I believe these actors gave up much too soon. They may have missed out on some great opportunities (and even greater careers) by listening to the wrong experts.

> "For every expert there is an equal and opposite expert."
> ARTHUR C. CLARKE

39. Don't Be Guilty by Association

"Without doubt, the most common weakness of all human beings is the habit of leaving their minds open to the negative influence of other people."
Napoleon Hill

There are a lot of actors out there—far too many—who simply cannot get out of their own way. They can never meet deadlines. They can never prepare properly for an audition. They can never stop complaining. They can never meet an industry person without saying or doing something completely inappropriate—and thereby obliterating that new connection.

Unfortunately, most of them are never going to do much of anything in our industry. Worse still, many will try to prevent you from doing anything in the business, either.

Misery loves company. And misery wants that company to be equally miserable with it. Avoid people who drag you down, belittle your dreams and ambitions, and are overly negative most of the time. This is not always easy to do. Sometimes, the one we need to avoid is a neighbor, coworker, or even a family member. There is a workable solution. Try to see that toxic person less frequently and for shorter periods of time. Don't accept every invitation to get together. When you must see them, try to arrive a little late—and be sure to have another engagement scheduled to attend afterward … so you can make a quick getaway if you need to.

It's even more important to avoid these negative characters at live auditions. The most difficult people you'll meet in Los Angeles, unfortunately, are even more unpleasant to be around in the waiting room at auditions. They'll talk incessantly, distract you from focusing on your script, and will make sarcastic, insulting, demeaning comments to the other actors—and sometimes even the casting directors and producers.

They'll also start complaining very vocally about traffic, the Dodgers, the casting director running late, and all the auditions they didn't get called in for. When the casting director steps into the waiting room, make sure you're not seated next to that problem person. That grumble-burger may be a very similar physical type to you. When the casting director pops in and out between the waiting room and the audition room, you can very easily be mistaken for the other actor if you're sitting next to one another. Don't take that chance. Get up and move to the other side of the room. Get up and step into the lobby or rest room. Remember to stay within earshot in case they call your name.

Put as much real estate as possible between yourself and a problem actor. Not just physical real estate, but mental real estate, as well. Go back and reread GiGi Erneta's audition experience in the foreword to this book. Put yourself in her shoes. What will you do to stay focused when you are in that same situation? How

---

How will you tune out the background noise and chatter when the stakes are high and the pressure is on?

> **Start thinking about what strategies you can develop to keep yourself focused and on track to win.**

will you tune out the background noise and chatter when the stakes are high and the pressure is on?

Start thinking about what strategies you can develop to keep yourself focused and on track to win. You don't have to get sucked into other people's negative energy. Don't be embarrassed to get up and change your seat. Learn to protect yourself and your mental space. Don't ever take a chance on being guilty by association.

> "Nine-tenths of the people were created so you would want to be with the other tenth."
> HORACE WALPOLE

40. Develop Legendary Patience and Focus

> "It's not the most brilliant that excels in film and writing, but the most patient."
> **MARTIN SCORSESE**

Become the most patient person you know. Become the most focused person you have ever met. The two most important qualities I believe actors—and people in general—really need to develop nowadays are patience and focus.

I learned the value of patience and focus early in life. In my teens and twenties, I trained hard and competed in "shoot wrestling" and "submission grappling." The goal was not to score a pin-fall but to make the other guy quit. Most of my training partners were bigger, stronger, and more experienced than I was. I never expected to beat any of them when I started. When we practiced, my plan was always the same: to hold them off for as long as possible before they beat me. That was the strategy I used to improve each week.

Something interesting happened. By developing patience and focus—while the other guys were building their killer instincts—I often beat wrestlers who were much better than me. Instead of trying to win, I went on defense and just tried to last as long as I could. With time, I became pretty good at defense, which frustrated the other guys more than I ever expected. As our matches wore on, they became angry, tired, and prone to mistakes—which I could then capitalize upon. My patience simply outlasted their hyperaggressiveness. I was surprised at how effectively this worked back in my younger days. Our coaches were surprised too.

When I started acting, I used this same defensive strategy in the waiting room at auditions. Other guys in my category would frequently play these aggressive little "mind games" in the waiting area, hoping to "psyche out" rival actors. Some of them were really good at it. Fortunately, I seldom got drawn into their drama and childish behavior. Instead, I focused on the script. I've made it a career-long habit, in fact, to study the script voraciously right up until the moment the casting director called me into the room. As a result, I sometimes discovered a little twist, nuance, or hidden clue in the script that I missed earlier … and made a last minute adjustment in the way I played the role. That tactic sometimes helped me book the role.

In contrast, the guys playing their little head games in the waiting area were focused on the other actors. What should they have been focusing on? The script, of course. By placing their attention on the other actors, they distracted themselves, became frustrated and angry, made mistakes, and blew their own auditions. Like my old wrestling opponents, they were too aggressive for their own good—and were complicit in their own defeat. Napoleon Bonaparte said it best: "Never interrupt your enemy when he's making a mistake." For the record, I never thought of the other actors in the room as enemies—but that was the way they treated me and the other guys reading for the same role. You don't have to have an enemy for an enemy to have you.

You don't have to have an enemy for an enemy to have you.

Remember the big picture. Remember why you came to Hollywood. Remember why you left the safety and security of home. Remember everything you've sacrificed to get here and stay here. Don't allow yourself to be pulled into other people's drama, chaos, and manipulation.

Develop the patience to concentrate fully on your script—and everything else you do for your career. Develop the focus to tune out all the distractions, background noise, and bad actors around you—in the audition room, in the Zoom room, in the gym, at your apartment complex, in traffic, at your favorite restaurant, at the coffee shop, in line at the bank—and everywhere you go in Hollywood. I promise these two qualities will do you a world of good in the entertainment industry capital of the world—and everywhere else your lives and careers may someday take you.

> "I learned many things working with Cary Grant. He has such tremendous concentration. Many actors do not have the courage to stand still. Cary Grant knows how to concentrate, how to look directly at you, but always with great relaxation."
>
> Sophia Loren

41. Never Do Stock

"People make troubles for themselves—no one forces them to choose boring jobs, marry the wrong person or buy uncomfortable shoes."
—Faina Ranevskaya

There are companies that pay actors to pose for "stock photographs." On the surface, this seems similar to hiring actors for a traditional commercial print job. It's not.

A print job is a still photo shoot in which actors and models are hired to portray characters in a print media advertising campaign. It's also called "real people modeling." It's similar to fashion modeling but with models of all ages, shapes, and sizes represented. The images are then used in billboards, newspapers, magazines, online advertising, and direct mail campaigns.

Print ads are a terrific resource, allowing actors to supplement their income with paying work that's closely related to acting in film, television, and theater. Even better, actors can put together a portfolio of the finished ads (called "tear sheets") to help establish credibility as working, bookable performers.

Stock photography, unfortunately, works a little differently. Stock photo companies will pay actors to pose for pictures in a wide variety of styles and settings—but without having any specific sponsor or client in mind to represent.

Actors can make a decent rate of pay for the day, but usually far less than they would earn in a traditional print campaign created through an ad agency. Stock photo agencies buy all rights to the images throughout all media "in perpetuity." Beware of that phrase "in perpetuity." It means "forever" ... leaving actors no option to renegotiate rights and terms at a later date. The stock agencies can also resell those pictures to any buyer, and for use in promoting any product or service whatsoever in the future. Anyone who can pay their price can buy your image.

Many actors have been burned when long-forgotten pictures they posed for early in their careers resurfaced, often at the most inopportune moments. Even if the pictures seem relatively tame—fully clothed in business attire, for example—they can someday be sold to a sponsor who is in direct competition to the company that just gave you your big break.

I heard a story years ago. It may be true—or it may be an old showbiz myth. A popular soap opera star had done a stock photo shoot early in her career. The head of the network was opening his mail one day and saw a picture of his daytime star in a cheesy direct mail ad for a laundry soap company. This was a different soap company than the one paying his network millions in advertising revenue each year.

The head of the network called the TV show's producer and read him the riot act. On Monday of the following week, the actress read her script and found that her character had a headache. By Friday of that week, the headache had developed into a brain tumor. By the following week, her character was killed off and written out of the show. The actress had forgotten all about that old photo shoot—but those images were still floating around out there and available for purchase.

Advertising agencies pay researchers big money to seek and find stock photos that can elevate the status of their high-paying clients. In situations like this, unfortunately, the popular soap opera star—who had made a bad decision early in her career—was considered expendable. Network television executives do not like to be embarrassed in public.

It can be tempting to go for the quick, easy money early in your career, but do yourself a big, big favor and resist this option. I never met an actor who did a stock photography shoot who didn't come to regret that decision later. But, as we used to say in the Bronx: "You can't unscramble those eggs."

Run, don't walk whenever you hear the phrases "stock photography," "throughout all media," and "in perpetuity." The opportunity cost will be far, far greater than whatever they're planning to pay you for the day.

> **"A sign of wisdom and maturity is when you come to terms with the realization that your decisions cause your rewards and consequences. You are responsible for your life, and your ultimate success depends on the choices you make."**
> **DENIS WAITLEY**

42. Don't Ask for Coffee

> "Common sense in an uncommon degree
> is what the world calls wisdom."
> SAMUEL TAYLOR COLERIDGE

This is one of those weird, very specific lessons you can only learn through experience. I was fortunate to learn this one secondhand—through the experience of a very talented screenwriter friend.

My writer friend landed an important meeting with a high-powered literary agent at a large, prestigious agency. He was very excited for the opportunity. This was the type of agent and office that could really help him get to the next level in his writing career. He arrived a little early and was well-prepared. He had notes on future projects he was creating, slick, well-produced documents for past projects he had written and sold, and a detailed list of questions for the agent.

The agent's assistant walked him into the office and let him know that her boss was running late. "He sends his apologies and will arrive shortly," she said. "Can I get you a beverage?"

My friend is a humble, down-to-earth, low-maintenance kind of guy. Like many writers, he's also very sensitive and a little socially awkward. He didn't want to be any trouble, so he just asked for coffee, thinking that would be the simplest option. Pour hot coffee into a paper cup. Boom. Done.

To his surprise, the assistant returned carrying a large silver tray with a fancy silver coffee pot with a long spout. There was a smaller silver pot with creamer and an elegant little dish with sugar cubes and silver tongs, a linen napkin in a silver ring, a beautiful place setting, and a porcelain cup and saucer with a fancy little doily in-between.

He was stunned. It wasn't what he expected at all. He told me later it felt like he was meeting the Queen of England for high tea. He suddenly found himself fussing with all these high-end props—that were way out of his comfort zone—and became a little bit frazzled.

A few minutes later, the agent arrived carrying a Starbucks cup! He looked at my friend juggling all these props and gave him a sour look. The meaning was unmistakable: "Why are you making my assistant jump through all these hoops when you're here to talk business with me?"

The two of them never got past that uncomfortable first moment. The meeting didn't go well, unfortunately, and they never worked together. You never get a second chance to make a first impression. Little things don't mean a lot. They mean everything.

Asking for coffee shouldn't normally be a big deal—except in that rare, one-in-a million instance when the request blows up in your face. This is an unusual example, but it points to a larger, more important issue: self-sufficiency. Ralph Waldo Emerson said it best: "The basis of good manners is self-reliance." You never want to be the person who always seems to require extra help or attention. You don't want to be "that guy."

> **You never want to be the person who always seems to require extra help or attention.**

If you absolutely must have something to drink, ask for water. Water will only arrive in a cup or plastic bottle. Anything else that someone brings you has the potential to be an unexpected x-factor that can interrupt you, break your focus, and totally get you off your game. Don't take that chance. Be as self-sufficient as you possibly can. This will show everyone around you that you don't need a lot of hand-holding and that you can be trusted on set—or in a writers' room.

> "The keenest sorrow is to recognize ourselves as the sole cause of all our adversities."
>
> SOPHOCLES

43. Don't Badmouth Your Agent

> *"When we speak evil of others, we generally condemn ourselves."*
> **Publilius Syrus**

You'll never attract a new agent by complaining about your current agent. Some actors make the mistake of badmouthing their agent all over town—including to the new agent they're interviewing. Apparently, these actors think the new rep will somehow take this as a challenge to work harder for them than the agent they're planning to leave.

Not surprisingly, this approach never works. The new agent may politely listen to your complaints. While listening, though, he'll be picturing you six months into the future—complaining to your next new agent about him! He may also be friends with the agent at the other office; they may know each other socially or have been coworkers at a different agency in the past.

Finding an aggressive, well-connected agent who believes in you and is willing to work hard on your behalf can be extremely challenging. Even star-name actors struggle with this issue from time to time. I know a gentleman who was an Emmy Award winner and a series regular on a popular network television show. He once told me that he was frustrated with his agent and often had trouble getting him on the phone! His agent, I believe, had simply become complacent; he was satisfied collecting big commission checks from this client but was not terribly motivated to seek out new opportunities while the show was still running and the money was still pouring in. Finding a great agent who will work with you to help build your career is one of the most challenging pieces of the Hollywood puzzle—but complaining about it won't help you through the process.

One of the most common reasons actors become frustrated with their agents is the belief that they don't have open lines of communication with them. It's a mistake, however, to think that signing with an agency gives you the right to call them whenever the mood strikes you. If you're looking for a guaranteed way to annoy your agent—picking up the phone to "call and check in" each week is a terrific way to do it. This shows agents their actors are needy and insecure—which works about as well in our professional relationships as it does in the dating world. Your agent is not your therapist. Your agent is not your mommy or daddy. Your agent did not fly down from Mount Olympus to solve every problem in your life.

Our agents are working hard to nail down audition appointments for us and all the other clients on their rosters. They do not appreciate the constant interruptions—and do not need to be reminded that their actors would like to be auditioning and booking more frequently. Our agents, by the way, would also like us to be booking more frequently—so they can collect more commission checks! You and your agent have the same goal.

An agent once told me that the best reminder to keep an actor at the forefront of his mind is a commission check crossing his desk. If you absolutely must call your agent, please call at the end of the day, preferably after 4:00 p.m. In the mornings and early afternoons, agents are racing the clock to send in their submissions before all the other agents they're competing against.

Many actors who are trying to be pro-active—but going about it all wrong—also make the mistake of calling to ask for feedback on the auditions they didn't book. This is a classic beginner's mistake. It tells your agent that you lack confidence in your audition skills and will require a lot of coddling and handholding. It also shows your agent you're oblivious, self-involved, and don't understand the day-to-day realities of their job. It indicates to agents that you don't realize how busy they are—and don't appreciate how hard they are working on your behalf.

Additionally, there are many variables and moving parts in the casting process. There are many reasons why an actor does not get the job—or even a callback. Casting directors will very rarely take the time to provide your agent with specific feedback on an audition you didn't book. Casting directors simply do not have the time—and are not interested in sharing information that may start a heated conflict.

Agents are also trying to be respectful of casting directors' time and patience. An experienced agent is smart enough to establish good boundaries with casting directors—and not bombard them with excessive requests. Actors should follow this example. Actors should treat their agents with the same common courtesy. Respect their time. Respect commonsense boundaries.

Always remember that we're in a people business. We can't be all things to all people. Not everyone will "get" us. But we all have personal autonomy over our lives. We can make a daily decision to conduct our business with intelligence, dignity, and respect.

> **Agents are also trying to be respectful of casting directors' time and patience. An experienced agent is smart enough to establish good boundaries with casting directors—and not bombard them with excessive requests.**

As artists, we need to remember to not only work on our craft, but also develop our interpersonal and business skills. There are several books in the recommended reading section(s) that deal specifically with these topics. *Swim with the Sharks* and *Skill with People* are two of the very best.

Please don't drive your agent crazy. Like actors, agents need to have thick skin, but you don't want to be the one actor on their roster who is continually testing its thickness. That's not the way you want to stand out with your agent. And never badmouth your representative in public—not even behind supposedly closed doors. Try your best to cultivate good relationships with all your representatives. If you feel that you're not working effectively with your agent or manager, then schedule an in-person meeting to talk it out. If the issues can't be resolved, then part ways amicably. Always do your best to take the high road in show business. It's much less crowded up there.

By the way, if you schedule a meeting with your agent somewhere outside their office, please be smart enough and gracious enough to pick up the check. An agent I know told me that one

> **Please don't drive your agent crazy. Like actors, agents need to have thick skin, but you don't want to be the one actor on their roster who is continually testing its thickness.**

of her actors recently invited her out to lunch at a nice restaurant. He showed up late, ordered the most expensive thing on the menu, then ordered a second meal to bring home for his wife—and then stuck her with the check. She's no longer his agent.

> "You must never lower yourself to be a person you don't like."
> HENRY ROLLINS

44. Don't Talk About Your Health Problems

> "Talk happiness. The world is sad enough without your woes."
> ELLA WHEELER WILCOX

Considering how obvious this one is, I'm always amazed at how many intelligent, high-functioning adults can't figure it out. I recently ran into an industry professional, an experienced writer-producer, who I hadn't seen in ten years. I made a big mistake. I innocently asked, "How are you?"

He proceeded to rattle off a very long list of his ailments, all the medications he's now taking, his upcoming medical procedures, and the shortcomings of his new insurance plan as compared to his old insurance plan.

Wow. His response was so extreme, I started looking for the hidden camera. I started looking for Allen Funt ... or at least Jamie Kennedy.

I invented a quick excuse to get away from him. By the time I figured out how to extricate myself from this one-sided, inappropriate tirade, however, I was completely exhausted. I felt like I had just gone fifteen rounds with Mike Tyson.

I hadn't seen this gentleman in ten years, and the first thing he did was start complaining and airing all his dirty laundry for me to see and hear and smell. He never once asked how I was

> **People in Hollywood will run from you if you give them any indication you lack the energy, vitality, and focus to be productive in our fast-paced industry.**

doing, by the way. If he had, I would never have responded the way he did.

Don't complain about your health issues to everyone you meet. We all have problems we're dealing with that we'd rather live without. However, it does nobody any good—least of all you—to go on and on talking about them. Les Brown, the great motivational speaker, explained this principle best: "Eighty percent of people don't care, and the other twenty percent are glad it's you!"

There's a practical application to consider here, as well. People in Hollywood will run from you if you give them any indication you lack the energy, vitality, and focus to be productive in our fast-paced industry. John Wayne had a much better approach. Speaking with an interviewer after his cancer surgery, the Duke said: "They ripped a lung out of me. I thank God I'm still here." John Wayne had the right idea. He was hopeful and optimistic for the future in spite of his dire circumstances in the present. More importantly, he expressed his hope and optimism verbally out in public.

Discuss your aches and pains with your doctor. Yapping about them with everyone else you meet just shows the world you're oblivious, self-involved, and ultimately incapable of rolling up your sleeves, focusing, and doing good, solid, productive work in our highly competitive, youth-oriented field.

> "The truth that many people never understand, until it is too late, is that the more you try to avoid suffering the more you suffer because smaller and more insignificant things begin to torture you in proportion to your fear of being hurt."
> THOMAS MERTON

45. Nothing Good Happens After Midnight

> "The belief in a supernatural source of evil is not necessary; men alone are quite capable of every wickedness."
>
> JOSEPH CONRAD

My father had a great saying: "Don't borrow trouble." There are a thousand things you can do in Hollywood that will get you into more trouble than you can possibly imagine—especially late at night. Staying home, making yourself a sandwich, and cracking open a good book will never get you in trouble. When in doubt, please stay home with the sandwich and the book.

Networking takes place during normal working hours—generally between the hours of 8:00 a.m. and 7:00 p.m.

Beware of networking events, after-hours parties, "once in a lifetime opportunities," "movers and shakers," "VIPs," and "cool people" who are only available to meet you late at night—and in non-traditional settings. Beware of private parties held at private residences in out-of-the-way locations. Beware of parties on boats and private planes. Beware of meeting people you don't know at their homes for "casting approval." Beware of meetings and auditions in hotel rooms. Beware of people who try to gain your confidence and get too friendly too fast. Beware of drinking beverages from open containers—that you did not open and pour for yourself.

Take precautions. And then take more precautions. And then take even more precautions. Trust your gut. If something doesn't feel right, it's probably not. There's usually a very good reason for that weird, uncomfortable feeling in the pit of your stomach. Always err on the side of safety. There are thousands of people in this city with less than honorable intentions ... to say the least. And there's a broken heart for every light on Sunset Boulevard.

Unscrupulous characters have been slithering around, preying upon hopeful Hollywood newcomers since the early days of our industry. None of this started with the "Me Too" movement, by the way. It's been going on for more than a hundred years. Will Rogers said it best: "In Hollywood you can see things at night that are fast enough to be in the Olympics in the day time." For a little historical perspective, take the time to research the story of Roscoe "Fatty" Arbuckle—one of the most successful, most talented stars of the silent film era—and the horrific scandal that ended his career.

When in doubt, bring a friend—preferably a friend with muscles. There's safety in numbers. Reputable people will meet you at legitimate networking events—which take place in safe environments during normal business hours. Nothing good ever happens for your career after midnight.

> **"The most important thing you can cultivate is the ability to listen to your intuition."**
> CHASE JARVIS

46. Make Friends with Procrastination

"Step by step and the thing is done."
Charles Atlas

We've all been guilty of procrastination. Generally, we procrastinate most on the things we most need to do. Anything that's new to us, outside our comfort zones, or just plain hard to figure out—these are the things people tend to put off most.

Don't beat up on yourself. You're not alone. As a species, this is how we're wired. Our subconscious minds work twenty-four hours daily to protect us. Your subconscious mind doesn't want you to challenge yourself. It doesn't want you to go to Hollywood—and have to figure out how to become a movie star, a millionaire, and a philanthropist. It wants you to avoid risk and danger, play it safe, find a mate, settle down, have kids, and keep on propagating the species.

That's why we encounter so much resistance anytime we try to roll the dice and accomplish something new and spectacular with our lives. And we encounter just as much resistance from ourselves as we do from family and friends. Our need for safety and security—as individuals and as a species—compels us to procrastinate. It's a deep-seated emotional need and is trying to protect us from hurt, pain, loneliness, isolation, rejection, failure, and bankruptcy. In the process, it's also insulating us from the potential upside of risk: those monumental successes possible when we set major goals for ourselves and take massive, focused action to achieve them.

Success is generally achieved in small, incremental steps. High achievers in every field tell us they accomplished great things through the discipline of developing regular, consistent work habits. British statesman Benjamin Disraeli summed it up best, explaining: "The secret to success is constancy of purpose."

Ironically, we can use procrastination as a tool to help practice the small incremental steps necessary for larger goal achievement. People who accomplish great things do it through regular, consistent daily efforts—even when those efforts are very small. In time, small steps add up in powerful and effective ways. Big doors swing on little hinges. In contrast, people who fail to achieve their goals generally do so because they look too long at the big picture and large, overall process. They become discouraged and overwhelmed—and never take that first small step. They give up before they even start.

How can procrastination help us? We can plan for it. We can recognize that procrastination will be a natural outgrowth of any worthwhile activity we pursue in earnest. We can factor procrastination into our daily equation. Make a list of ten or more goals you wish to accomplish in the entertainment industry—or even in your personal life. Make your goals as specific as possible. Break those goals down into manageable, easily digestible steps. Small steps always work best. Develop the habit of getting into action with small, bite-sized chunks of effort every day. Then, whenever procrastination kicks in—as it inevitably will—switch over to your next goal and apply another bite-sized chunk of effort.

Remember, our aim here is not to fight procrastination. We're just trying to outsmart it and outrun it for a while. We can do this by consistently applying the technique of bite-sized chunks

> **By taking small steps daily towards each goal, you'll bring yourself progressively closer and closer to accomplishing all your goals over time.**

of effort to a wide range of goals—both personal and professional. By taking small steps daily towards each goal, you'll bring yourself progressively closer and closer to accomplishing all your goals over time.

You can use this strategy indefinitely, moving from one task to the next, and constantly staying one step ahead of procrastination, inertia, and overwhelm. This technique will get you into action and help keep you there. It will help you avoid burnout while making small, incremental changes and advancements in multiple areas of your life simultaneously. And when you start to see the results of all the tiny, bite-sized chunks of effort you put into your acting career (and your personal life) bearing fruit ... you'll have procrastination to thank for it.

> "I do small things. I try to do good things every day."
> JACKIE CHAN

47. Act Right

> "Beginning today, treat everyone you meet as if they were going to be dead by midnight. Extend to them all the care, kindness and understanding you can muster, and do it with no thought of any reward. Your life will never be the same again."
> — OG MANDINO

This might seem like common sense, but common sense—like common knowledge and common courtesy—is sometimes not so common. Every stranger you meet is fighting some kind of battle. No matter what kind of day you're having—and no matter what else is going on inside your head—you can make a conscious decision to smile, be friendly, and say a kind word to every person you meet. At minimum, please try not to increase another person's stress level.

Practice smiling before you walk out your door. This may sound overly simplistic, but it's worth our attention. Los Angeles is filled to overflowing with people scowling so deeply, I often think they're competing for the Blue Ribbon of Grumpiness. However, there is no Blue Ribbon for Grumpiness. There never has been. It doesn't exist. When you're the grumpiest person in Hollywood, the price you pay is rejection, failure, loneliness, and isolation.

Ironically, being friendly to someone who's having a bad day may help you pull yourself out of your own rotten mood. This one should be obvious—but unfortunately, it isn't. There are many people in Hollywood who go out of their way to annoy those around them.

Maybe it's stress. Maybe it's frustration. Maybe it's one-upmanship. Maybe it's a desire to make themselves feel relevant by harassing, antagonizing, and inconveniencing others. Whatever it is … don't do it. And, if you've been doing it, stop doing it. Author Paulo Coelho said it best: "Don't allow your wounds to transform you into someone you are not."

Let me provide three examples of how people in this city misbehave. There are people who will get your name wrong … then intentionally keep calling you by that wrong name on purpose—even after you've corrected them several times. I don't have too many pet peeves, but this is one of them. This has happened to me more times than I care to remember … and there aren't too many names easier than "Mike."

Example two. One afternoon, I was in a large office building for an audition. I was in the restroom down the hall from the casting office—along with two other actors who were reading for roles in the same project. When the first one finished "his business," he exited … but made sure to shut the light and the door on the way out! He left me and the other actor in the restroom in the dark!

My favorite example, though, is hard to believe until you experience it for yourself. You're in a crowded parking lot looking for a spot. You see a car getting ready to leave. You pull up and wait. Then … the other driver doesn't leave. He won't leave his parking space if he sees someone waiting for it. He'll make phone calls, clean the dashboard, organize his glove box … and anything else to keep you from taking his parking spot. The goal is to delay you until you give up in frustration and drive away … and then he'll finally leave.

The first time I experienced this I was stunned. I thought I had a pretty thick skin. I had just arrived in Hollywood from New York and was going to dinner with two friends who had lived here for many years. I pointed out that the other driver was inconveniencing himself just as much as he was inconveniencing us. I'll never forget my friend's explanation: "No. He's happy just knowing he's making us miserable."

Be aware that you will encounter characters like this. They go out of their way to irritate and inconvenience others. They exist. They're out there. Make sure you avoid them when you see them. More importantly, make sure you never see one of them staring back at you when you look in the mirror. This world is round. What goes around comes around. The person you harass, annoy, and antagonize may be sitting across the desk from you at your next meeting or audition.

Abraham Lincoln understood this principle well. Lincoln was sad, lonely, and depressed for much of his life. Prior to winning the White House, his law partner often found Lincoln hunched over at his desk first thing in the morning—rocking back and forth, with his head buried deep in his hands. These were unmistakable signs of hopelessness and despondency. Lincoln was *personally pessimistic* about the world and all its problems. Among people, however, Lincoln was friendly, soft-spoken, and enjoyed telling jokes and funny stories. He made a lifelong commitment not to focus on his own challenges, but to improve the world for others before leaving it. Lincoln dedicated himself to making life better and brighter for others before checking out.

Don't worry. You don't have to set the bar nearly that high. It's not your job to save the Union. Just make a commitment to be friendly, cordial, and gracious to every person you meet. Try it today. Then try it again tomorrow. Then the next day. Then the next. Then keep going until it becomes your new daily habit.

If you're really having a bad day, please stay home. You should never drive angry anyway. Negative energy just attracts more negative energy. Please don't go out and about in Hollywood with a bad attitude and a mammoth chip on your shoulder. Though Los Angeles is a very big city, you'll find that this industry is a surprisingly small circle. Treat everyone you meet—in or out of our industry—with courtesy, dignity, and respect. Almost everyone here in Hollywood is doing something in the industry here in Hollywood. Not all actors are going to stay in the actor lane throughout their careers. The person you interact with casually today could be directing their first feature film tomorrow. Do your best to make that interaction a positive one.

The last thing Los Angeles needs is another grumpy actor. Make a decision not to be that actor. Be better, not bitter.

> **"Even if you're unhappy, just pretend that you're happy. Eventually, your smile will be contagious to yourself. I had to learn that. I used to think, 'I'm being fake,' but you know what? Better to be fake and happy than real and miserable."**
> **EVANGELINE LILLY**

48. Recharge Your Battery

"If I thought about it, I could be bitter, but I don't feel like being bitter. Being bitter makes you immobile, and there's too much that I still want to do."
RICHARD PRYOR

Sometimes we have to recharge our batteries. We have to step away from it all, reboot, refresh, and take a little time off. We have to take time to smell the roses—and not just hit the poses.

This is important if you're feeling stressed or overwhelmed—signs you may need a little break. There's no shame in taking time off when you need it. Sometimes we have to take two steps back to get a running start.

You don't have to spend a lot of money to recharge your battery, either. Remember, you're living in the second largest city in the U.S. and the entertainment industry capital of the world. There are all kinds of resources available to help reignite that creative fire within and remind yourself why you're pursuing this business in the first place.

Here are a few ideas:

1. Go to a live taping of a TV show. It still amazes me how many actors in Hollywood have never attended a live TV taping. Ideally, you should try to see a network sitcom being filmed with a three-camera set-up. You will learn a lot about our industry watching a sitcom being taped in real time. It's often difficult

to get tickets for the most popular shows. If you can't find your way onto a studio lot to watch a sitcom, then you may enjoy sitting in the audience for a talk show or game show taping. Those are great second choices. I promise you will learn a lot—and the experience will inspire you.

2. Walk up and down Hollywood and Vine, scope out the star names engraved on the sidewalk, and familiarize yourself with a few of the old-time greats. Research their careers and try to find a star from fifty (or even a hundred) years ago whose background is similar to your own. Keep looking until you find someone who really resonates with you—someone who will inspire you and whose career you would like to emulate. I bet you won't have to look too hard.

3. Spend an afternoon visiting stars of yesterday in their final resting places at Hollywood Forever Cemetery, Westwood Memorial Cemetery, or Forest Lawn. Remember that all of them —no matter how rich and famous they became—probably got frustrated with different aspects of our business too, maybe even at the height of their careers. They all had their ups and downs. They all lost money—sometimes in the millions. They all were overlooked for jobs. They all felt unappreciated and disrespected at times. They all had their hearts broken. Think about how little those problems and challenges would matter to them if they were alive today—and available to buy you a cup of coffee, sit down and answer all your questions, and become your best friend, mentor, and confidante.

Don't be afraid to take a little time off. This industry will still be here when you get back. Show business can be a pretty rough game. Don't compound it by being unnecessarily tough on

> **If you take a little time off now, you may not feel the need to quit the business later …**

yourself. Don't beat up on yourself. Your career is a marathon, not a sprint. Recharge your battery when you feel you need it. In the long run, you'll come back stronger and you'll last longer. If you take a little time off now, you may not feel the need to quit the business later—like some of my old friends and castmates did when things suddenly became too difficult for them to bear (Secret 38: The Experts Aren't Always Right).

For the record, experienced actors will tell you that if you plan a little trip out of town to decompress, you will inevitably get a call for an important audition. I've found that the best way to get a last-minute audition when things are deadly slow is to buy a non-refundable plane ticket. I'll gladly take the loss on the airline ticket; I'd much rather have the audition. The good news is that your audition may be just the thing you need to reignite your creative fire and get you back in the game again.

> "Almost everything will work again if you unplug it for a few minutes, including you."
> ANNE LAMOTT

49. A Lesson from *The Duck Factory*

> "There will come a time when you believe everything is finished; that will be the beginning."
>
> LOUIS L'AMOUR

Many years ago, I had a favorite television show that aired on Friday nights. It featured an unknown, long and lanky funny-man who was one of the most talented comedic actors I had ever seen. I thought this young actor was the modern-day successor to Charlie Chaplin, Buster Keaton, and Harold Lloyd. He starred in a short-lived sitcom on NBC called *The Duck Factory*. I looked forward to that show every week ... and used to ask myself, "Why have I never heard of this guy before?"

The Duck Factory only lasted one season. It never found its wings—or its audience. I remember thinking to myself, "Wow ... Hollywood is such a tough place to be. Even a terrific comedic actor like that guy ... in a wonderful, wildly inventive comedy like *The Duck Factory* ... just couldn't make it in that highly competitive television market."

I forgot all about that show until six years later—when *In Living Color* aired on Fox TV and propelled Jim Carrey into the Hollywood stratosphere. Like many of our favorite stars, Jim Carrey was "an overnight success" who took many years to get there. But imagine if he had allowed himself to become demoralized after *The Duck Factory* was canceled. That would have been a reasonable response to what must have been a tremendous disappointment to

It's reasonable to expect that any kind of reasonable success in Hollywood is going to take an unreasonable length of time.

him at the time. Imagine all the wonderful work we never would've seen from Jim Carrey if that immensely talented young man had gone back to his native Canada with his tail between his legs after his first TV show was canceled.

Very often, actors give themselves an artificial time limit for success. I've heard so many good actors over the years say, "I'm gonna give it three years, and if I don't make it by then, I'll go back home and settle for Plan B."

Giving yourself a time limit for success in show business never made much sense to me. It's very difficult to predict how long the seeds we plant will take to bear fruit. It's reasonable to expect that any kind of reasonable success in Hollywood is going to take an unreasonable length of time. Don't give up on your dreams just because of the time you think it may take you to accomplish them. Those years will pass anyway—whether we use them to advance our careers or not.

Besides, your definition of success will differ from mine—and both of ours will differ from Jim Carrey's. We can probably ask a hundred different actors and get a hundred different definitions of what it means to "make it" in Hollywood. I had a discussion on this topic with several of my closest actor and writer friends. Some of them defined success in Hollywood as the ability to make a decent living from their acting and writing entirely—and without having to work at a survival job any longer. Through a little honest introspection, these friends were pleasantly surprised to discover that—by their own definition—they had already "made it."

I believe actors should be prepared to stay in the game for as long as it takes to build our credits and establish ourselves. There are many factors outside our control, such as the recent union strikes and pandemic lockdowns, that can adversely impact our short-term productivity.

It's a good idea to use an unintended work stoppage as an opportunity to plan, strategize, take new headshots, create new marketing materials, take classes, learn a new monologue, update your demo reels and casting profiles, attend networking events, and find creative ways to stay productive. Having a long-term perspective is the best way to keep ourselves focused and on track when the short-term interruptions wreak havoc upon our lives and career plans. Maintain a long-term perspective as best you can. This mindset will help you weather all the inevitable storms in Hollywood.

For the record, I believe that even if *In Living Color* had flopped, Jim Carrey would have bounced back again and found another pathway to monumental success. That guy was absolutely unstoppable. I'm pretty sure he never gave himself an artificial deadline to "make it."

> "I went in the Marines when I was sixteen. I spent four and a half years in the Marines and then came right to New York to be an actor. And then seven years later, I got my first job."
> GENE HACKMAN

50. The Clock Is Ticking

> "For a long time it had seemed to me that life was about to begin—real life. But there was always some obstacle in the way, something to be gotten through first, some unfinished business, time still to be served, a debt to be paid. Then life would begin. At last, it dawned on me that these obstacles were my life."
>
> **ALFRED SOUZA**

There's no earthly reason all of us can't accomplish much more than we do—and in a far shorter period of time.

One of the best friends I ever had was Johnny Valiant, a world renowned pro wrestler. He became an accomplished actor, stand-up comedian, and stage monologuist after his wrestling career was over. Johnny was one of the funniest, friendliest guys I ever met. He had thousands of great stories about his worldwide travels—and was a truly gifted storyteller. He even wrote and performed a one-man stage show, "An Evening with Johnny Valiant," packed with wonderfully entertaining stories and anecdotes of his adventures in the ring and on the road.

All of that is a fantastic recipe for a book.

I talked with Johnny about writing a book several times but wish I had talked about it more. He lost his life in a freak accident back in 2018. I'll never read Johnny's book because I never pestered him enough to write it. I know it would have been sensational.

If you want to accomplish something truly extraordinary with your life—and I'm guessing that's why you moved to Hollywood—then get yourself into action today. A good plan executed today is much better than a perfect plan executed next week. Aim for progress, not perfection. Start today, not tomorrow. Remember, the clock is ticking daily for every one of us—even celebrities and world class athletes. Time moves quickly. It also seems to speed up as you get older. The years don't wait around for anyone.

Twenty years ago, I was hired to teach a beginner acting class for senior citizens in a Los Angeles nursing home facility. I will never forget the experience. I taught there for two years and got to know many of these older adults pretty well. I was invited to holiday parties at the facility and met many of my students' children and grandchildren. Most of the senior citizens in my class were happy, friendly, outgoing people. They were extroverts who enjoyed the new challenge of a weekly acting class. They had fun performing with their friends each week.

Several other residents, unfortunately, had personal stories that were absolutely heartbreaking. And what was most heartbreaking for me was that their stories were always the same. They would wait until class was over and then ask to speak with me privately. They would become very uneasy, start looking down, wringing their hands, and shuffling their feet. Then they would confide in me that they had wanted to try their hands at an acting career when they were eighteen, nineteen, or twenty years old. They had performed in pageants, talent shows, stage plays, commercials, and radio dramas as children and teenagers. They had received a great deal of early encouragement from teachers, coaches, and directors. One of them had even performed on

The Arthur Godfrey Show, a popular, nationally broadcast television program that was the predecessor to *Star Search* and *America's Got Talent* way back in the 1940s and 1950s. Arthur Godfrey was considered a "king-maker" back in the early days of television.

Unfortunately for these aspiring young performers, family, friends, coworkers, and romantic partners all talked them out of pursuing their Hollywood dreams. I found that it was always those same four culprits—family, friends, coworkers, and romantic partners—who convinced my students to pursue more practical, more stable careers and lifestyles instead. My students dutifully complied. They settled down. They got "real" jobs. They got married. They raised families. They forgot all about their early, impractical show business dreams—just as they were instructed to do.

Along the way, though, they frequently asked themselves: "What if?" And then, after working for fifty years in a variety of other professions, they showed up in my acting class at the nursing home. They told me they had spent the last five decades—and sometimes six—wondering how life might have been different if they had been more protective of their youthful goals and aspirations. Not only were they sad and remorseful as older adults, they had also grown cold and bitter about the wasted, lost years and missed opportunities. They were angry and sarcastic in their scene work and the exercises we performed. They would argue with me when I tried to offer positive feedback and direction in class.

Interestingly, as well, the first few times I heard these senior citizens' stories, I would "zone out" and start thinking about my old castmate Bob Horen (Secret 8: There Are No Small Parts). Bob spent fifty years working in the entertainment industry rather than fifty years regretting the decision to give it up. He didn't spend fifty years beating up on himself. He spent fifty years making the most of himself. Ralph Waldo Emerson said it best: "Make the most of yourself, for that is all there is of you."

Sometimes, it's the people closest to us who stand most solidly in our way—and stop us from moving forward towards the goals and desires that will fulfill us most. This is a hard truth to accept. There are many well-meaning dream stealers and dream killers out there in the world. I'm guessing Bob Horen had people like that in his life too when he was getting started—but that he chose not to listen to them. Some of us, unfortunately, also have people in our inner circle who may not really have our best interests at heart. Don't let other people steal your dream. Your dream was given to you, not to them.

Anthony Robbins says there are two types of pain in life: the pain of discipline and the pain of regret. Please don't spend the next fifty years of your life asking yourself: "What if?" There are a hundred things you can do in Los Angeles to build your credits and your career without having to ask anyone's permission—even without an agent, big money, or major credits. One of the best ways to catch an agent or manager's eye, in fact, is to create your own opportunities. Write your book. Make your movie. Launch your podcast. Put together your web series. Start your theater company. Perform your one-person show. Create your own work.

Author John Mason says we can't turn back the clock, but we can rewind it every day. This is a great way of thinking that we can easily apply to the entertainment industry. Examine your own long-term dreams and goals. Is there something you've wanted to do—in or out of show business—that's fallen by the wayside?

Completing a neglected project from yesterday will boost your confidence and do wonders for your self-esteem.

Ask yourself if you're now willing and able to go back and bring that early goal to fruition. Maybe there was a good reason for not completing that project at the time. More importantly, maybe your timing is a little better right now.

People wait all week for the weekend, all year for the summer, and all their lives to be happy, successful, and productive. There's an old saying: "The best time to plant a tree was twenty years ago. The second best time is right now." Completing a neglected project from yesterday will boost your confidence and do wonders for your self-esteem. A little extra confidence and self-esteem will always give you a competitive edge in Hollywood.

Start that project today. Don't put it off for another year. Next year may be one year too late. The clock is ticking daily for all of us.

> "People don't run out of dreams.
> People just run out of time."
> GLENN FREY

Afterword: Give It Your All

> *"What I observed about my fellow actors was that most gave up very easily."*
> HARRISON FORD

There's a tendency for artists to believe that everyone we meet has it all figured out—except us. This is probably just human nature, but it's an aspect of human nature that can really trip people up. It can discourage people and make them feel so overwhelmed that they give up before they even get started.

Don't give up. Give it your all. Kick your career into high gear. Don't let "potential" be written on your tombstone. I've come to the conclusion that nobody really fails in show business. But most people make the decision to quit much too soon.

I'm a firm believer that not everyone can be a star—but everyone can develop their skills, learn their craft, familiarize themselves with the Hollywood rules, and slowly begin to build their credits and careers. Everyone can prepare themselves and train themselves to book substantial speaking roles in this industry.

And if you should someday decide—after giving it your all—that you don't want to pursue an acting career any longer, then you can move on to Plan B with no regrets. Believe me, as you grow older, you'll appreciate the freedom and peace of mind that come with looking back on your life with as few regrets and excuses as possible. You'll always remember that you had the

Give this business everything you've got. Watch what happens for you when you stop holding back.

courage to follow your heart, step up to the plate, and participate fully in one of the most competitive industries on this planet.

If you get just one thing out of this book, I hope it is this: I hope you will make the decision to put distractions aside and give it your all. Give this business everything you've got. Watch what happens for you when you stop holding back.

I wish you all the best of happiness and success—in and out of show business.

Now go get 'em.

> "I remember when I was about eighteen, Sean Penn made a bet with me. He had just directed his first movie, and he's like, 'By the time you're thirty, I will bet you five hundred dollars that you'll be sick of acting.' I'm still waiting to collect, because I'm not."
>
> **WINONA RYDER**

Appendices

"The things you get fired for when you're young are the same things that you get lifetime achievement awards for when you're old."
Francis Ford Coppola

A Suggestion for Younger Actors

> "The young do not know enough to be prudent, and therefore they attempt the impossible—and achieve it, generation after generation."
> PEARL S. BUCK

If you're an actor in your twenties or thirties, you're in a truly enviable position. This has always been a youth-oriented industry. Agents and managers will be much more likely to give you a chance because they know you (potentially) have many productive years ahead of you. If you are a solid, bookable young actor with great acting chops, strong audition skills, and a good head on your shoulders, they know they'll be able to work with you—and earn big commission checks—for many years to come. That's the good news.

On the negative side, there's an unfortunate stereotype about young actors in our industry. Agents and casting directors think young people know all about current trends in our business. Young people know everything about the latest films, television shows, and star-name actors—but know very little about those from years ago. This is unfortunate because our industry has such a rich, diverse, and fascinating history.

If young actors will take the time to research films, television programs, and popular stars from years ago, I think you'll be pleasantly surprised at how much you enjoy the experience. In fact, I think young actors should make this a regular practice. This should

Mike Kimmel

Successful projects always generate a number of copycat projects.

be a part of your actor training. Do this every week and watch what happens. I'm guessing you'll discover a whole new set of favorite actors who lit up the screen before your parents were even born. You'll find movies and television shows from years ago that remind you of your modern-day favorites. There's a good reason for this, because directors and producers often pay tribute to movies, TV shows, and plays that inspired them when they were younger.

Successful projects always generate a number of copycat projects. Creators in our industry are always looking for films, television programs, books, and plays that are well-received in the marketplace so they can identify new trends and capitalize on them financially. The goal is to piggyback off their successful, proven formulas—and their excellent timing with viewers. This is not a lack of creativity. This is business, pure and simple. Studios and networks want to make money.

With the success of Clint Eastwood's *Unforgiven* in 1992, producers thought Westerns were hot again. They started asking: "Where are our Western scripts? Do we have any Western directors? Which actors look good on a horse?" Similarly, *Saving Private Ryan's* success in 1998 created a great deal of interest in war movies, particularly stories about World War II. HBO's *Band of Brothers* was one of the better results of this renewed interest.

Even back in the 1950s, *I Love Lucy* was so popular that television producers started scrambling to duplicate its success. One of the better "knockoffs" was *I Married Joan*, which NBC rolled out in 1952—just one year after *I Love Lucy* premiered on rival CBS. It was a terrific sitcom starring Joan Davis, a truly gifted comedienne, in the Lucille Ball role. Her husband was played brilliantly by Jim Backus—who most of us will remember as the millionaire on *Gilligan's Island* and the cartoon voice of Mr. Magoo. Unfortunately, *I Married Joan* only ran for three seasons and has been largely forgotten. As you can imagine, it was pretty difficult for any show to compete against *I Love Lucy* back in the day. All these years later, not many shows have even come close—but I give a lot of credit to the producers and cast of *I Married Joan* for giving it the old college try.

You will impress agents and casting directors if you can talk intelligently about an obscure movie or television show from the 1950s—or a top actor from that generation—and then relate them to better-known current-day projects. You'll show agents and casting directors that you're not just another young person walking around glued to your phone. You'll present yourself as someone with a good understanding of the history of our industry. This will set you apart from the other young actors in your category. Demonstrating this type of long-term perspective and industry knowledge will help you stand out from the crowd with agents and casting directors—especially those with a little grey in their hair.

> **"The generation gap is within the person who thinks there is a generation gap."**
> DR. MAXWELL MALTZ

Mike Kimmel

A Suggestion for Older Actors

> "I think we are able to keep active provided we approach our lives with creativity. I think the mere fact that we keep doing is self-creating."
>
> JESSICA TANDY

If you're in your forties, fifties, or beyond, and just getting started as an actor, I believe you have a tremendous opportunity. Yes, this is a youth-oriented industry, but your own life journey has been different. That makes you unique. This is the next phase of your life—and you can make it a remarkably successful and rewarding one. A useful strategy is to keep asking yourself: "How can I use this?" Ask yourself daily how you can turn your age—and each of your life experiences—into a plus rather than a minus.

Put yourself in the shoes of a seasoned agent or casting director interviewing actors. Do a deep dive into your own life, prior work history, and personal story. Find the aspects that will be most interesting to these industry professionals in conversation. Remember, these people have interviewed hundreds of actors fresh out of drama school. They've heard it all before. They know all about the classes, workshops, and experiences of well-trained newcomers. They've met dozens of actors who've performed Shakespeare in the Park. They know that world very well.

They don't know your world. They haven't met you. Your background is different. You can use it to really pique their interest. Your travels, job history, maturity, financial stability, interpersonal skills, and other unique life experiences may be incredibly interesting to them. Find ways to accentuate your most engaging and dynamic past experiences—and be sure to discuss all of these in your meetings and interviews.

Through the years, I've worked with many performers who started acting in their forties and beyond. Some of them retired early from careers in other industries with pensions and fascinating life stories—but zero credits in the acting world. Nevertheless, they were able to capture the attention of industry professionals, land good speaking roles, and build respectable second careers later in life. Most of these "late bloomers" were also very good at figuring out their types—and playing roles that were closely related to their actual former careers.

Several well-known stars, in fact, started out later in life. Dennis Farina retired from his career as a Chicago police officer—and transitioned beautifully into playing cops, detectives, and criminals on screen. Danny Trejo ran with the wrong crowd early in life, but used that experience—and his incredible tough guy looks and persona—to play those same tough guy characters in major films. Dennis Farina and Danny Trejo are two of the best known, but there have been many others who started late in life and achieved great success, including Kathryn Joosten, Morgan Freeman, Ken Jeong, John Mahoney, and Michael Emerson. Author Barbara Sher said it best: "It's only too late if you don't start now."

My mother, Rose Kimmel, started acting at age seventy. Mom was a natural extrovert who genuinely loved people. I saw firsthand how much those qualities endeared her to agents and casting directors. They didn't care that she didn't go to drama school or have a long resume. These industry professionals appreciated her enthusiasm and saw her as a fresh face in the senior citizen category. For the previous ten or fifteen years—whenever they needed an elderly female—they saw the same ten or fifteen ladies in their offices. Some of these veteran performers had been working and auditioning for fifty years and had very solid skills. Some, unfortunately, had also become a little jaded, bitter, and grumpy through the years (See Secret 47: Act Right). All of a sudden, my mother started showing up at their auditions with her bubbly personality, willingness to learn, and can-do attitude. Again, put yourself in the shoes of a seasoned agent or casting director. Which elderly female would you want to hire? It didn't take long for my mother to start booking commercials and print, join the Screen Actors Guild, and land a nice supporting role as Jerry O'Connell's mother in MTV's first live-action feature film, *Joe's Apartment*.

They didn't care that she didn't go to drama school or have a long resume.

Just because you're starting late doesn't mean you're starting empty. Your past does not equal your future. Don't let past experience color your future expectations. Your prior work history (Dennis Farina) and life experiences (Danny Trejo) can be incredibly valuable in this industry—and can easily translate to bookings and dollars when presented with insight and ingenuity. Just because you've never worked as an actor doesn't mean you can't; it only means you haven't (yet). We can change so much through diligence and focused effort that we won't even recognize our former selves six months from now. Opportunities exist for those willing to find them—and create them.

Throughout this book, we've discussed the value of creating your own work. This is even more important for mature actors because you'll be competing against actors in your age group with substantial credits and long resumes. The clock is ticking. You have a tremendous opportunity, but you'll need to start catching up. You'll need to build credits for your resume and footage for your demo reels. That should now be your primary focus.

An effective way to accomplish both these things is by rolling up your sleeves and shooting your own short films. Team up with friends in your acting classes and put together a plan to make this happen. Find other friends who are interested in writing, directing, lighting, camera work, sound, and editing.

When planning your short film projects, keep your scripts as short as possible. Short films have a tendency to develop an aggressive life of their own—and often end up being much longer than intended. One page in a script generally translates to one minute on screen. A ten-page film script, unfortunately, can often stretch into a fourteen or fifteen-minute long film. Once your film starts approaching the twenty-minute mark, it's becoming too long.

You'll have a far better chance at getting your project accepted into festivals if you can keep its total running time under ten minutes. FYI, if you can shoot a good short film that is between one and three minutes in length, the film festival programmers will love you. They will see your project as a great choice when planning out their schedules. They can position your three-minute film in between two of the longer films to keep the audience interested and the program running smoothly. Keep it short. The shorter the better. You'll be accepted into many more festivals if your film is shorter.

Most importantly, when you create your own short films, you can write roles for yourself that highlight your special skills and most marketable physical characteristics. You can use the footage for your demo reels. You can submit your finished projects to film festivals worldwide. You may even become an award-winning filmmaker in the process. (Some of the smaller festivals only have three or four entries in certain categories. It's not too difficult to become a winner or runner-up.)

This process will help you build your credits and your career in a practical and systematic way. It will get you in motion and help keep you there. Best of all, it will show agents and casting directors that you're new to this business, but your life experience has made you a go-getter—and not just another grumpy actor sitting around complaining about his agent and waiting for the phone to ring.

> **"Life is available to anyone no matter what age. All you have to do is grab it."**
> ART CARNEY

A Challenge for Acting Teachers

> "I was discouraged at drama school, along with most of my peers."
> **SIGOURNEY WEAVER**

I've worked in several smaller markets, where there is a hard separation between the theater actors and their local counterparts in television and film. Theater actors in these markets will not audition for on-camera roles, and the TV-film actors never work on stage.

This is a monumental mistake. Though the techniques we use are different, actors do not need to choose between performing on stage or on screen. The best actors adjust their technique and are able to go back and forth effortlessly between the two mediums. In theater, our movements are bigger and our gestures more pronounced so audiences can see us from the back row. On screen, our movements are much smaller and more intimate—so we're not over-the-top when performing for viewers one-on-one in the privacy of their living rooms.

Experienced actors in the larger markets—Los Angeles, New York, and Chicago—are equally comfortable performing in both worlds. Our industry is far too competitive for actors to limit themselves to any one type of venue (Secret 29: Be Flexible. Be Adaptable. Be Bookable.). As actors, we need to work on broadening our horizons, not restricting them.

Laurence Olivier didn't believe he had to choose between the stage and the screen. Considered one of the greatest of modern-day actors, Olivier made his reputation performing Shakespeare on stage in London. His film work was equally impressive—from his sociopathic villain in *Marathon Man* to his delightful comedic romp with Marilyn Monroe in *The Prince and the Showgirl*. He operated seamlessly between stage and screen, comedy and drama, throughout his career. Between his many diverse theater and film roles, Laurence Olivier was also smart enough to make mountains of money shooting Polaroid commercials here in the States. Sir Laurence didn't think commercials were beneath him, and he certainly didn't turn his aristocratic British nose up at those mammoth residual checks.

Anthony Hopkins, Judi Dench, Meryl Streep, Jennifer Garner, Al Pacino, Dustin Hoffman, Steve Martin, Martin Short, and most of our favorite stars do exactly the same. They perform brilliantly in both mediums—and that's what you and I should do, as well. Acting teachers, particularly those in the smaller markets, can help their students achieve long-term success by teaching them to transition fluidly between stage and screen—and helping them remove arbitrary, regionally-imposed limitations. Teach your students to approach our industry like the stars do—and like the very best working actors in the larger markets do—and you will be setting them up for successful, long-term careers.

Acting teachers, especially those in four-year college drama programs, can also help their students succeed by giving them an immersion in real world situations and audition scenarios. There is simply no substitute for real-world experience. It's common knowledge among working actors that what we don't

There is simply no substitute for real-world experience.

know can really hurt us in the audition room—and on set. There's also a stereotype in our industry that there's a separation between theory and practicality in many acting classes—especially in our colleges and universities. Just as there should be no separation between working on stage and screen, there should also be no separation between practical and theoretical applications for student actors in class.

Many young actors graduate from four-year college drama programs with terrific skills and a thorough knowledge of the acting craft. That's an excellent foundation for our business (Secret 30: Theater Credits Count). A frequent complaint among working professionals, however, is that these programs often do not prepare students to compete in television, film, and commercials; they only prepare them for careers in regional theater. Most of their college instructors themselves, in fact, have only worked professionally in the theater. While this is a challenge for teachers, it is one that can be addressed and overcome with planning, focus, and an open mind.

It would be a good idea for teachers to start dropping some of our fifty secrets into their curriculum. Teachers can start opening up the room for practical discussion questions with their students. You'll find discussion questions and ideas based upon these fifty secrets in the next section. Good teachers can add many more discussion questions of their own. The human mind is a problem-solving mechanism—much like a computer. Posing thought-provoking, practical questions in your acting classes will open up young actors' minds to finding real solutions and starting their careers off on the right foot.

Teachers can also bring in guest speakers with strong television and film credits—and real world experience from the New York, Chicago, and Hollywood trenches—to assist in preparing young acting students from colleges and universities to compete in the real world. Don't be afraid to reach out to busy, working actors. Never be intimidated by a guest speaker's professional credits. Most importantly, don't be reluctant to introduce your students to a classroom guest with stronger professional credits than your own (Secret 28: Beware the Green-Eyed Monster).

There's an old African proverb: "If you want to go fast, go alone. If you want to go far, go together." The stage and screen are collaborative mediums. None of us individually is as capable as all of us working together on behalf of your students. Experienced working professionals who visit your class are not your competitors—they're your collaborators.

For the record, working actors understand how challenging your job can be. They have tremendous respect and appreciation for what great teachers are able to accomplish in the classroom. Many working actors—despite their strong credits—will also admit that they would have no idea how to teach an acting class. Just because someone has a particular skill set doesn't mean they are qualified to teach that skill to newcomers. Great acting teachers are worth their weight in gold. They are a tremendous blessing in this industry—especially those with the best of intentions and the smallest of egos. Working film and television actors

---

Don't try to be the most popular teacher for your students; try to be the most effective teacher for your students.

---

who visit your classes can learn just as much from you as your students will learn from them. It's a win-win for all of us.

Don't try to be the most popular teacher for your students; try to be the most effective teacher for your students. In the performing arts world, teachers can accomplish this by helping to prepare their students for the real world challenges they will encounter in the audition room for professional jobs—both on stage and on screen.

> "I decided to take a stab at acting. I entered the American Academy of Dramatic Art, where one teacher told me I'd never make it—I was too tall."
> FRED GWYNNE

Discussion Questions and Ideas for Further Study

Secret 1: The Best Actor Doesn't Always Get the Job

Have you ever had a dry spell like Eddie's? How long would you be willing to stay in the business without booking a job? Six months? One year? How do you think Eddie kept himself going during the lean months and years?

Do you have a physical characteristic that has previously worked against you in life? How you can you use this trait as a plus rather than a minus in your auditions?

Do you have a headshot that highlights that trait? Ben Painter, a young student of mine, is a mixed-martial arts fighter with a prominent cauliflower ear. He was smart enough to show off that ear in his headshots—and it helped him book several film roles. Like Eddie's "unusual profile," Ben's cauliflower ear has turned out to be a moneymaker for him. What can be a moneymaker for you?

Secret 2: Sometimes the Answer Is "No" Before You Even Walk Through the Door

Can you imagine a scenario in which you auditioned for a job that was not even available? What would you do if the best audition of your career was for a job like that? Do you think you may have already been in that situation without knowing it? Can you imagine a strategy that would help you if that situation were to come up sometime in your career? How would you deal with a situation like this?

Secret 3: Some Will See You as a Threat

How can you identify an agent who may be trying to "shelve" you? Have you ever been contacted out of the blue by someone and then wondered "How did this person find me? Where did they get my number?" What are some potential warning signs? How can you do some background research to protect yourself?

Secret 4: Don't Sign Across the Board

Why would an agent want you to sign across the board? How will you respond when an agent insists that you sign across the board with their office? In which area of the business do you think you are most likely to earn the most money for your agents? Which area of the business are you most interested in pursuing? How can you keep your focus on that primary career goal? Can you create a target list of people you want to work with in that category? Who would be on that list? How will you contact them and follow up?

Secret 5: Expand Your Radius. Widen Your Circle.

Can you handle the rigors of the road? Where can you realistically be a local hire? Do you have friends and family you can visit in nearby markets? How far are you willing to drive for an audition or booking? How far is too far for you? What is the minimum pay rate you are willing to accept for an out of town job? How much money do you need to break even? Are you willing to lose money traveling to another city for a good acting job—just to build your credits?

Secret 6: Nobody Cares What You Drive

Money is an excellent servant, but a terrible master. Don't let it control you. Are you overly concerned about status and "keeping up with the Joneses?" Where do these ideas come from? Are you good at keeping your expenses under control? Do you spend less than you earn? Can you get better at this? How can you cut down on your everyday and monthly expenses? Do you have a savings and investment plan in place? Have you ever sat down and made yourself a budget? Do you know someone who can assist you in this area?

Secret 7: Get a Job

Do you have a job that offers some flexibility to allow for auditions and bookings? What skills do you have to earn money outside our industry? What can you do to protect yourself financially and remain solvent—no matter what is going on in the entertainment industry? Most experts agree we should maintain enough of a cushion to pay our bills for at least six months if we lose our jobs. How much of a financial cushion do you need? Can you find a "side hustle" to bring in a little extra money once in a while? Your side hustle can slowly turn into a solid, full-time income stream.

Secret 8: There Are No Small Parts

When you're new to the industry and your credits are light, it's helpful to build your resume with smaller roles. Have you ever turned down a role because you thought it was too small? Many experienced actors will choose to turn down a smaller role on a new TV show because they're hoping for a bigger role later in the season. This can be a risky choice. The show may be cancelled before a better opportunity comes around for you.

What can we learn from the story of Bob Horen? How good are you at creating interesting backstories for your auditions and roles? How can we create strong backstories for our supporting characters—while still honoring the context of the script and without overshadowing the lead players?

Secret 9: You're a Type. Know it. Own it. Nail it.

Do you know your type? Do you know your age range? Ask people whose opinions you can trust. An exercise I use in my acting classes is to have each student take turns sitting in a chair quietly at the front of the room. The rest of the class writes down all the different roles, occupations, ethnicities, and nationalities they think you can realistically play. You can try this with a group of friends too. You'll be surprised at what comes up. We don't always see ourselves the way the rest of the world does.

Secret 10: Don't Change Your Look

How do people see you? Is your look marketable? What type of wardrobe best supports your look? What are your best colors and styles? Would you consider changing your hair color and length? Do you want to change your body type? Would this make you more marketable? Do you have people in your circle you can trust to advise you before making any changes? Will you schedule an in-person meeting with your agent or manager before making a change?

Secret 11: Don't Disqualify Yourself

Are there other roles you think you can play outside your normal type? Joe Pesci is on the shorter side—and doesn't have big, bulging muscles—but always manages to play a convincing tough guy or mobster. How does he accomplish this? Do you ever practice different walks, gestures, or mannerisms for characters you're portraying? Get in the habit of asking yourself, "How would this character walk? Can I adjust my speech tempo or cadence? How can my body language and mannerisms enhance my portrayal of this character?" This is how British actors train, by the way. They tend to work "from the outside in," rather than "from the inside out."

Secret 12: Take a Stage Combat Class

Do you exercise regularly? Are you physically fit? Do you know how to work around your physical limitations and injuries? Have you ever had to perform a fight scene on stage or screen? Did you work with a skilled fight choreographer? Do you have any actor friends who are experienced in this area? Can they suggest a beginner's stage combat class for you?

Secret 13: Ask Them to Show You

Have you ever been asked to do something on stage or screen that you knew could be dangerous? How did you respond at the time? What would have been the ideal response in that situation? How can a sense of neediness or "people-pleasing" lead us into potentially dangerous situations on set? How can we all do better next time?

During the filming of *Total Recall*, Arnold Schwarzenegger was asked to swing from a length of drapery and crash through a double glass door. Just because he was Mr. Olympia, they assumed he could swing through the air like Tarzan and crash through glass. He looks like he pull it off, doesn't he? Fortunately, Arnold had the good sense to ask for a little coaching—and a stunt double. If it could happen to a mega-star, it could happen to us. Stay safe out there.

Secret 14: Keep Your Shirt On

Do you have strong boundaries? As a viewer, how do you feel about gratuitous nudity when you see it on stage and screen? Are you comfortable with your body? How will you react when someone crosses the line with you? It's always helpful to be prepared for these situations before they come up. Don't let them catch you by surprise. Do you have a few ready-made responses to inappropriate comments and suggestions? Practicing techniques of verbal self-defense is just as important as practicing physical self-defense.

Secret 15: Don't Take the Bait

What are your temptations? What do you have trouble resisting? How can you prepare yourself when these temptations arise during the day? What strategies can you develop to help you remain focused and productive? Do you have trustworthy friends you can call in a pinch? Do you need professional help or counseling to kick a bad habit? Don't be embarrassed to seek out professional help if you need it. No matter what temptation you're struggling with, there are plenty of effective resources out there that can help. You're not alone, I promise.

Secret 16: Don't Become a Groupie

Do you tend to be overly impressed with people's celebrity status? Have you met and interacted with a celebrity—or a family member of a celebrity? Do you have healthy boundaries with the people you meet? Are you a people pleaser? Do you have trouble saying "No"? Are you good at recognizing unreasonable requests when people send them your way? What are some good responses you can prepare for when people cross the line with you?

Secret 17: Learn to Compartmentalize

Have you ever been publicly embarrassed by someone you considered a friend? How did that happen? How can you avoid those situations in the future? Do you have people in your life with poor social skills? Have you seen some of your friends and neighbors behave badly in social situations? Do you know people who are abrasive and difficult to get along with? Can you think of some situations where it would be wise to keep these people in their proper lanes—and be careful not to introduce them to your trusted team members?

Secret 18: Don't Slurp Your Soup

Do you have good manners and social skills? Are you able to interact effectively with all types of people—no matter their income, position, or perceived social status? Do you know some people who are very good at this? What can they teach you? What can you learn from spending more time around them? Start aiming higher.

Secret 19: Two Ears. One Mouth. Do the Math.

Are you one of those people who always has to be the center of attention? Be honest with yourself. Do you have a tendency to dominate conversations with others? Do you interrupt and talk over other people? Start thinking about what you may be missing when you don't pay closer attention to those around you. You may be missing out on pearls of wisdom that can change your life for the better. You may be missing out on mentorship that can get you to the next level in your career.

Secret 20: Master the Fine Art of Listening

Good acting is reacting. Are you a good listener? How can you improve in this area? What potential benefits would this bring you in your scene work? Start watching movies and television shows and look for this particular skill in your favorite actors. Notice which stars are better at this than others. Al Pacino and Scarlett Johansson, I believe, are two of the very best. They have so much going on in their eyes while their costars are speaking. I can watch their "silent dialogue" for hours and never be bored.

Secret 21: Not Everything Requires Your Response

Can you think of a time when you talked too much in public and embarrassed yourself or those around you? Have you seen other actors behave this way? Have you noticed the way others react around these overly self-involved actors? What are these actors missing? How can you avoid making these same mistakes in the future?

Secret 22: You're Not a Walking Resume

Are you a walking resume? Are you always talking about yourself, your credits, your bookings, your travel, your possessions, and your accomplishments? How do you think this affects people who interact with you on a regular basis? Do you know some other actors who fit this description? What would be more interesting topics of conversation for all of us? What can we do to become better conversationalists? How can we start today? What would be a good first step? Who is a good role model for you in this area?

Secret 23: Use Your Voicemail

Learn to protect your time and mental energy. Do you have people in your life who are time wasters and "energy vampires?" Do they keep you from meeting deadlines and finishing projects? Can you find ways to spend less time around these people? Are you the smartest, most ambitious, hardest-working actor in your circle? How can you "step up your game" and find access to a higher functioning group of friends and coworkers? Do you schedule alone time to think, plan, and reflect? Do you set specific goals for yourself? Do you keep a journal to track your progress?

Secret 24: Watch Your Language

Do you curse? Do you regularly have to edit yourself and be careful that there are no children nearby when you're speaking with other adults? Do people have to remind you to watch your language? Has this been a recurrent issue in your life? Do you think you can start making a change in this area? Can you see the benefit in cleaning up your language? Do you think cursing may have cost you jobs or opportunities in the past? Can you remember a time in the past when someone visibly cringed because you dropped an F-bomb?

Secret 25: Your Hand Can Shake You Right Out the Door

Are you stuck in that old-fashioned mindset of shaking hands with every person you meet? Have you ever thought about where this idea comes from? Different industries have different industry standards. Can you understand why shaking hands can be a bad idea in our industry? Are you able to adapt? Are you willing to change this habit?

Secret 26: Don't Stink Up the Room

Do you wear perfume or cologne every day? Do you feel under-dressed and uncomfortable in public if you are not wearing perfume or cologne? Where did you get this idea? Have you been overly influenced by social pressure or Madison Avenue sales tactics? Advertisements for perfumes and colognes are slick and sexy—and can be very convincing. Try to see through the slickness of their ads and notice the thinness of their actual content. What steps can you take to become more resistant to advertising and social pressures to conform and follow the crowd?

Secret 27. Pay Attention. Eyes Open. Head on a Swivel.

Do you have good instincts? Do you notice when things are not quite right and people seem a little bit off? Remember the advice of Henry James: "Try to be one of those on whom nothing is lost." Can you take a hint when industry people seem uninterested in what you have to offer? Do you know how to exit a room quietly—and without drawing too much attention to yourself? Can you think of some ways in which a little more attention in this area can be helpful in the long run?

Secret 28. Beware the Green-Eyed Monster

Do you have a scarcity mentality when it comes to money and opportunity? How can we start working to overcome that? What would be a healthier mindset for you? How do you react when a friend books a great job? Are you genuinely happy for that person? Do you feel envious—even when your friend is a different physical type than you? How about when the roles are reversed? Are your friends genuinely happy for you when you score a major victory? Can you tell when they're not?

Secret 29. Be Flexible. Be Adaptable. Be Bookable.

Which area of the business do you feel is your strongest? In which area do you book most frequently? Do you turn down auditions in other areas where you feel less qualified—or simply less interested? What if the areas you were least interested in turned out to be the areas in which you booked most regularly? How can you adjust to that possibility? Can you think of ways to make yourself more marketable for the type of projects you are most likely to book?

Secret 30. Theater Credits Count

Are you experienced on stage? Have you ever been part of a large ensemble cast? What does the theater section of your resume look like? Do you enjoy working on stage—or is that just a means to an end for you? What skills can you learn from stage work? How can you start building your theater credits? Do you have a dream role you would like to play on stage?

Secret 31. Overcome Skepticism with Specificity

How can you highlight your strongest credits and most marketable physical characteristics on your resume? How can you demonstrate them to your best advantage in your marketing materials and on social media? Have you seen anyone who is really good at this? What can you learn from their example?

Secret 32. Be Mega-Prepared

On a scale from one to ten, how good are you at preparing for your auditions? Be honest with yourself. How can you improve in this area? Be specific. Can you make a commitment to work on this daily? What steps can you take today to get started? Do you believe this approach will help you improve your booking ratio? Do you need to buddy up with an accountability partner? How good are you at memorizing lines? Do you think the suggestions in this chapter can help you improve? What else can you do to improve in this area? Go out and buy yourself some index cards and different color pens. Trust me. It will be the best five dollars you'll ever spend for your career.

Secret 33. Practice Never Makes Perfect

Are you a perfectionist? Do you know people who never want to do something until they know they can do it one hundred percent right? Those are the people who never get around to doing anything. You've got to be willing to get out there and do it wrong so that you can learn how to do it right—or at least do it better.

Have you ever "no-showed" for an audition? This is a prime example of how perfectionism can work against our best interests. Hockey great Wayne Gretzky was right when he said that we miss one hundred percent of the shots we don't take. What can we do to overcome perfectionism before it overcomes us?

Secret 34. Think like a Producer

Do you understand the concept of thinking like a producer? Producers are professional problem solvers. What does this mean to you? How can you apply this principle in your daily life? Do you think you can use this mindset to start booking more work? What type of acting jobs can you envision that would benefit most from hiring actors who train themselves to think like producers?

Secret 35. You Should Write Something

What is your background in writing? How comfortable are you with the writing process? When was the last time you sat down and wrote something—and then actually completed it? Many adults have not written anything since high school or college. What would be your preferred format—theater or film? Would you write a comedy or a drama? What genre interests you? Do you have a group of friends and colleagues you can collaborate with to produce your finished script? How can you connect with people outside your normal circle to collaborate with on your personal passion project?

Secret 36. Get Used to Criticism. You Will Get It.

What is the most unfair, unjust criticism you have ever received? How did you react? How can you improve on this response in the future? How helpful would it be to train yourself to thicken up your skin and become immune to unfair criticism? What are some steps you could take today to begin preparing yourself to deal with criticism and disrespect? Do you know some actors who have quit the business because they could not handle being criticized?

Secret 37. The One-Strike Rule

Have you ever had a high level, potentially life changing audition, meeting, or interview? How well do you think you typically perform in high stress settings? What might be some effective ways to prepare yourself for a meeting like this? Have you ever practiced "mock interviews" with your actor friends or in class? This is a great exercise to help you and your actor friends get comfortable interviewing with agents and managers.

Secret 38. The Experts Aren't Always Right

Do you give too much credibility to "experts" in our industry? Have you considered that they might be wrong—and may not know everything there is to know about the entertainment industry? Have you ever felt that you have been misjudged or poorly evaluated? What is the worst advice you've ever received from an expert? How can you train yourself to become the world's greatest living expert on you?

Secret 39. Don't Be Guilty by Association

Are you good at maintaining distance from problematic people? Are you good at identifying those people when you encounter them at auditions and industry events? How can you become better at avoiding conflicts and protecting your boundaries? Have you allowed difficult, toxic people into your inner circle? Are there people in your life who shouldn't be in your life? How can you start limiting your interaction with these people? How can you begin to disassociate yourself from these people without causing additional conflict and drama?

Secret 40. Develop Legendary Patience and Focus

Who is the most patient person you know? Who is the most focused person you know? Can you give some examples of how they demonstrate these qualities? What can you learn from them? What benefit does their patience and focus bring them in their day-to-day lives and careers? How can you start demonstrating these same qualities in your own life? Can you start today? What results do you believe these actions may bring you in the future?

Secret 41. Never Do Stock

Have you ever done a stock photo shoot? Can you tell the difference between a casting call for a traditional print job and a casting call for a stock photography shoot? (The stock photo shoot does not have a specific client in mind. The photos will later be leased out—potentially to many different clients. The actor will only receive a one-time payment.) What are the pitfalls and potential negative consequences of this type of work? Why would an actor choose this type of job? Why should an actor avoid this type of job?

Secret 42. Don't Ask for Coffee

Were you surprised at my friend's coffee experience in the agent's office? Clearly, his idea of a cup of coffee was very different from that of the agent's assistant. In what other ways can our expectations differ from those we encounter in professional settings? How can we anticipate these differences? How can we prepare ourselves more effectively when our expectations don't line up with those of others? What are some ways we can train ourselves to be more self-sufficient?

Secret 43. Don't Badmouth Your Agent

What expectations can we reasonably have when signing with a new agent? What do you think an agent's expectations are for the actors on their rosters? How can we verbalize our expectations effectively? How many auditions should we expect each week? How can we maintain good communication with our agents? How can we cultivate good relationships with our agents—so that things do not turn sour in the future? If we are not working well with our agents, how can we correct course and try to salvage the relationship?

Secret 44. Don't Talk About Your Health Problems

Do you complain about your health problems? Do you talk too much about your old sports injuries? What does this tell people about you? How do you react when other people talk endlessly about their aches and pains? How will agents and casting directors feel about working with an actor who seems to have poor energy and many unresolved health issues? Do you think they will be excited about working with a person like that? Will they be concerned that the actor won't have the energy to handle acting jobs that require long hours, multiple takes, and a great deal of memorization? Do you think they will have confidence in that actor for roles that are very physically demanding?

Secret 45. Nothing Good Happens After Midnight

How late do you usually stay out at parties and industry events? Are you always the last one to leave? Do you frequently go out to bars and clubs? What type of people do you encounter in these settings? Do you have good instincts to protect yourself in unfamiliar surroundings? Do you have good friends you can trust to accompany you to locations that don't feel safe? Have you ever taken a self-defense course? There are plenty of great options to study and train here in Los Angeles. In some neighborhoods, you can find a gym or martial arts studio on practically every block. What other steps can you take to stay safe and protect yourself?

Secret 46. Make Friends with Procrastination

Do you consider yourself a procrastinator? How can you start using our natural tendencies to procrastinate to your advantage? Can you see the benefit of working on multiple projects simultaneously—and then switching from one to the next whenever you feel the inevitable pull of procrastination? Once you get started on a project, how good are you at taking action, meeting deadlines, and accomplishing goals? How can you improve in this area? What action steps can you take today? Can you see the benefit of "bite-sized chunks" of effort? Would it help you to team up with an accountability partner?

Secret 47. Act Right

How are your social skills? Do you have people in your life who are abrasive and difficult to get along with? Do you know actors who behave poorly in public? Where do you think these actions come from? Do these actions stem from frustration with our business—or can you think of another explanation? How do you think the attitude of these actors affects the day-to-day results of all their efforts? How do you think the actions of these people reflect upon you?

Secret 48. Recharge Your Battery

Have you ever felt like you needed to take time off and take a break from it all? Are you able to handle the frequent highs and lows, ups and downs of our business? Do you have good friends and a solid support system in place? When you're feeling down, are there places you can go that always seem to inspire you? Have you been to some of our wonderful museums here in Los Angeles? Do you know a few good places for day trips to inspire yourself—and help get your creative fire back?

Secret 49. A Lesson from *The Duck Factory*

How do you think Jim Carrey felt when his first television show was cancelled? How do you think he coped and bounced back? How much more difficult would this process have been if he did not have a strong support system? What would you have done in his place? How many actors would have given up and quit the business if this had happened to them? Do you know some other actors like this? How long should it take to become an "overnight success?" Have you given yourself an artificial deadline to "make it?" How would you define "making it" in show business? What is a good definition of success for you? Does your definition of success differ from that of your closest friends and classmates?

Secret 50. The Clock Is Ticking

How much more could you accomplish if you worked to the best of your ability? How much more could you accomplish if you lived up to your potential? What would the best possible version of you look like, think like, sound like, and act like? What can you do to kick your career into high gear? How can you start today? What are the "baby steps" you can take right now to begin? Are there any longtime excuses or bad habits you need to eliminate? How can you start working towards those goals right now?

Recommended Reading

> "When I have a little money, I buy books;
> and if I have any left, I buy food and clothes."
> DESIDERIUS ERASMUS ROTERODAMUS

We had a saying in New York: "If you ever have to choose between buying a meal and buying a book, always buy the book. The meal will feed you for a day, but the book may feed you for a lifetime."

I'm an avid bibliophile. I am one hundred percent addicted to books—and have been for most of my life. As a kid, books kept me out of trouble in the Bronx. In high school, college, and beyond they helped me fill in the gaps between what my teachers knew and what I wanted to learn. As a middle-aged and older adult, they help me become more diligent, focused, and productive each day.

Books contain the wisdom of the world and the experience of everyone who has traveled this path before us. With the wealth of material now readily available to all of us, there is no excuse for being unprepared and under-informed. I'm including a list of my favorite titles in the entertainment industry. Several of these were not specifically written for actors, but give us wonderful insights into all the different aspects of our industry.

Acting for Films and TV by Leslie Abbott

Acting in Film by Michael Caine

Acting in Television Commercials for Fun and Profit by Squire Fridell

Actions: The Actor's Thesaurus by Maria Calderone and Maggie Lloyd-Williams

The Actor's Life by Jenna Fischer

Adventures in the Screen Trade by William Goldman

The Alchemy of Acting: The Evolution of Craft in Film by Jim Blumetti

All About Me by Mel Brooks

An Actor Prepares by Constantin Stanislavski

An Agent Tells All by Tony Martinez

The Art of Acting by Stella Adler

Audition by Michael Shurtleff

The Backstage Actor's Handbook by Sherry Eaker

Being an Actor by Simon Callow

A Book by Desi Arnaz

The Business of Acting by Brad Lemack

Catching the Big Fish by David Lynch

The Courage to Create by Rollo May

The Dramatic Writer's Companion by Will Dunne

Dreams Into Action by Milton Katselas

Ego is the Enemy by Ryan Holliday

Entertainment in the Old West by Jeremy Agnew

Fame: The Hijacking of Reality by Justine Bateman

Film: An Illustrated Historical Overview by Andrea Gronemeyer

Film and Television In-Jokes by Bill van Heerden

The First Frame by Steve McCarten

Screenplay by Syd Field

Free Play: Improvisation in Life and Art by Stephen Nachmanovitch

The Godfather Notebook by Francis Ford Coppola

The Great Movies by Roger Ebert

Greenlights by Matthew McConaughey

The Hidden Persuaders by Vance Packard

Hollywood by Charles Bukowski

Hollywood Babylon by Kenneth Anger

The Hollywood Survival Guide for Actors by Kym Jackson

How I Made a Hundred Movies in Hollywood and Never Lost a Dime by Roger Corman

How to Act and Eat at the Same Time by Tom Logan

How to Audition on Camera by Sharon Bialy

How to Avoid the Cutting Room Floor by Jordan Goldman

How to Get Ideas by Jack Foster

How to Make it in Hollywood by Linda Buzzell

How to Write a Movie in 21 Days by Viki King
Impro by Keith Johnstone
Improvisation for the Theater by Viola Spolin
In Such Good Company by Carol Burnett
It Would Be So Nice if You Weren't Here by Charles Grodin
Know Small Parts by Laura Cayouette
Leading with My Chin by Jay Leno
Live Cinema by Francis Ford Coppola
Love, Lucy by Lucille Ball
Making Movies by Sidney Lumet
Making Movies Work by Jon Boorstin
Meeting of Minds by Steve Allen
Mighty Minutes by Jim Hall
Movie Speak by Tony Bill
The Movie that Changed My Life by David Rosenberg
Much Ado About Me by Fred Allen
My Rendezvous with Life by Mary Pickford
Notes on the Making of Apocalypse Now by Eleanor Coppola
Number One is Walking by Steve Martin and Harry Bliss
Ogilvy on Advertising by David Ogilvy
On Screen Acting by Edward and Jean Porter Dmytryk
The 100 Greatest Advertisements by Julian Watkins

Mike Kimmel

100 Years, 100 Stories by George Burns
Peg Entwistle and the Hollywood Sign Suicide by James Zeruk Jr.
A Pictorial History of the Silent Screen by Daniel Blum
The Power of Myth by Joseph Campbell
A Practical Handbook for the Actor by Melissa Bruder
Purple Cow by Seth Godin
Reading the Silver Screen by Thomas C. Foster
Rebel Without a Crew by Robert Rodriguez
Sanford Meisner on Acting by Sanford Meisner
Social Media for Actors by Heidi Dean
The Talent Code by Daniel Coyle
Tips: Ideas for Actors by Jon Jory
True Strength by Kevin Sorbo
Understanding Movies by Louis Giannetti
A View from the Middle by Larkin Campbell
Who is Michael Ovitz? by Michael Ovitz
Wild Bill Wellman: Hollywood Rebel by William Wellman Jr.
Wishful Drinking by Carrie Fisher

> "We are like books. Most people only see our cover. The minority read only the introduction. Many people believe the critics. Few will know our content."
> — EMILE ZOLA

A Note on Self-Care

"The actor has to develop his body. The actor has to work on his voice. But the most important thing the actor has to work on is his mind."

STELLA ADLER

Artists, and actors in particular, are generally more sensitive and emotional than those pursuing other career paths. These are exactly the qualities that attract people to the performing arts in the first place. Many actors, however, often experience a deep sense of loneliness and isolation—far more than others in the general population. Many actors admit to feeling a vague sense of discomfort and "not fitting in with the crowd."

Unfortunately, the sensitivity that makes us good actors can also make us feel fragile and vulnerable out in the real world. I've known (too many) brilliant actors through the years who struggled with feelings of stress, anxiety, and depression. When left unchecked and unexplored, these feelings can rapidly spiral downward into deeply held beliefs of unworthiness and poor self-esteem.

Even our favorite movie stars can experience these challenges. No matter how rich, famous, and talented they may be, when people do not feel good about themselves internally, none of the external trappings of success—the money, the mansions, or the Maseratis—will make them feel any better. Happiness is an inside job.

Acting on stage and screen is an extraordinary thrill, but it's definitely not the right career choice for everybody. The frequent rejection and uncertainty of a show business lifestyle can be extremely challenging. Performers without powerful self-esteem, a strong sense of purpose, and a solid support system can have great difficulty navigating the day-to-day realities of our industry.

The best actors I know always seem to have a positive and optimistic outlook on life. They make it a habit to work on self-esteem and self-development strategies daily. They approach their own self-care and internal work with the same strategic diligence they use to develop their acting skills through the years—and break down audition scripts each week.

Experienced actors work hard to keep their minds and attitudes in great condition—just as experienced athletes hit the gym regularly to keep their bodies in tip-top form. This is a daily discipline. Most veteran actors will tell you they have a favorite book or two to assist them with this process.

The good news is that you don't have to read a thick college textbook on psychology. Hundreds of wonderful writers have made it their life's work to make these ideas accessible for all of us. They've created practical, substantive material to change people's lives for the better. Their books tend to be short, clear, and concise. They are easy to understand because they are meant to be applied directly to the everyday challenges in our lives. The following is a list of my favorite self-help and personal development books. I hope you will find a new favorite here, as well.

Studying human psychology helps actors discover layers, nuances, and depth of meaning in the characters we portray. It helps us discover subtext in our scenes and monologues. Psychology was never meant to be a purely academic pursuit; it's a practical discipline that helps us understand ourselves (and others) more effectively. There is an additional benefit to studying psychology and human behavior. We learn to develop and strengthen our own minds. By doing so, we can achieve a sense of mastery and control over our emotions.

Though this is a topic that is not typically discussed in actor training, I believe it needs to be. Anything that will help you as a person is also going to help you as an actor. I hope you will take this advice to heart—and delve deeply into one or more of the books on this list.

These books are intended to be self-help, not "shelf help." They are tools, but even the best tools must be used to have a positive effect in our lives. The novelist Ralph Ellison said it best: "Without the possibility of action, all knowledge comes to one labeled 'file and forget.'" A book can work wonders for us—but only when we take it off the shelf, read it, and apply it diligently to our own life situations. Make this a life-long practice in your own life. Start today. Build a better you.

As a Man Thinketh by James Allen

The Attractor Factor by Joe Vitale

Believe You Can by John Mason

Can't Hurt Me by David Goggins

The Charisma Myth by Olivia Fox Cabane

The Conquest of Happiness by Bertrand Russell

Do One Thing Every Day That Scares You by Robie Rogge

Don't Sweat the Small Stuff by Dr. Richard Carlson

Ego is the Enemy by Ryan Holiday

Emotional Intelligence 2.0 by Travis Bradberry and Jean Graves

Feel the Fear and Do it Anyway by Susan Jeffers

The 5 Second Rule by Mel Robbins

The Four Agreements by Don Miguel Ruiz

The Game of Life and How to Play It by Florence Scovel Shinn

Get Out of Your Own Way by Larry Winget

Grit by Angela Duckworth

How Successful People Think by John Maxwell

How to Stop Worrying and Start Living by Dale Carnegie

How to Win Friends and Influence People by Dale Carnegie

The Laws of Human Nature by Robert Greene

The Magic of Believing by Claude Bristol

The Magic of Thinking Big by David J. Schwartz

Man's Search for Himself by Rollo May

Man's Search for Meaning by Viktor Frankel

The Master Key System by Charles Haanel

Meditations by Marcus Aurelius

Mindset by Carol Dweck

The Obstacle is the Way by Ryan Holiday

100 Ways to Motivate Yourself by Steve Chandler
The Pocket Muse by Monica Wood
The Power of Now by Eckhart Tolle
The Power of Optimism by Alan Loy McGinnis
The Power of Positive Thinking by Norman Vincent Peale
The Power of Purpose by Joseph Leider
The Power of Your Subconscious Mind by Dr. Joseph Murphy
Psycho-Cybernetics by Dr. Maxwell Maltz
The Secret of the Ages by Robert Collier
The Secret to Conquering Fear by Mike Hernacki
See You at the Top by Zig Ziglar
Skill with People by Les Giblin
The Strangest Secret by Earl Nightingale
*The Subtle Art of Not Giving a F*ck* by Mark Manson
Swim with the Sharks Without Being Eaten Alive by Harvey Mackay
Think and Grow Rich by Napoleon Hill
13 Things Mentally Strong People Don't Do by Amy Morin
Thoughts are Things by Prentice Mulford
Tools of Titans by Tim Ferriss
The Ultimate Secrets of Total Self-Confidence by Dr. Robert Anthony
Wake Up & Live! by Dorothea Brande

The War of Art by Steven Pressfield

What to Say When You Talk to Yourself by Shad Helmstetter

You Can Be Happy No Matter What by Dr. Richard Carlson

You'll See It When You Believe It by Dr. Wayne Dyer

> "I was in darkness, but I took three steps and found myself in paradise. The first step was a good thought, the second, a good word; and the third, a good deed."
> FRIEDRICH NIETZSCHE

About GiGi Erneta

GiGi Erneta, born in New York City to Argentine parents, is an actress, broadcaster, and multidisciplinary artist with a career spanning over 30 years in film, television, and media. She began as a dancer, training with the Royal Academy of Dance and the British Academy of Dance, before transitioning to acting. At age fifteen, she booked her first SAG TV commercial, and later earned an acting scholarship to the University of Texas at Austin, where she graduated with a bachelor of science degree in radio-television-film. Post-graduation, GiGi worked at NASA's Public Affairs Office, collaborating with McDonnell Douglas on the International Space Station program. She produced engineering photography and media content, including images used by astronauts during Space Shuttle missions.

In film, GiGi starred in the award-winning military drama, *Flag of My Father*, playing Captain Judith Rainier, John Schneider's sister and William Devane's daughter. Additional feature film credits include the psychological thriller *When the Bough Breaks*, with Morris Chestnut, and the *Happy Death Day* franchise, a horror-comedy series grossing over $125 million globally per Box Office Mojo.

On television, GiGi has performed recurring roles in series such as *Roswell, New Mexico* (The CW), *The Purge* (Season 2, USA Network), *VEEP* (HBO), *The First* (Hulu), *Dallas* (TNT), *Veronica Mars* (UPN/CW), and Spanish-language telenovelas including *La Ley del Silencio*. On television, Erneta took on a lead role as Kelly Evert, a game ranch owner, in the faith-based drama *Sons of Thunder* (Pure Flix), showcasing her ability to anchor a character-driven narrative. Her guest roles include *Nashville* (ABC), *Jane the Virgin* (The CW), *American Crime* (ABC), *Scandal* (ABC), *NCIS: New Orleans* (CBS), *Friday Night Lights* (NBC), and *Strong Medicine* (Lifetime). She portrayed Jennifer Sawyer in the festive romantic comedy *Holiday in Santa Fe* (Lifetime), a story of cultural traditions and unexpected romance starring Mario Lopez. She also played George Jones' wife, Nancy Sepulvado, in the acclaimed limited series *George & Tammy* (Showtime), showcasing her dramatic range opposite Michael Shannon and Jessica Chastain. Additionally, she appeared in the neo-Western *Outer Range*.

Recently, she played Martha opposite Emma Stone, Nathan Fielder, and Benny Safdie in *The Curse* (Showtime/A24, 2023—present), a comedy-drama where her guest star performance earned Emmy consideration. She also recurs as Phillipa Verdi in *Vindication* (Season 4, Angel Studios), for which she also earned Emmy consideration. She also appeared in David E. Kelley's *Love & Death* (HBO Max), a true-crime drama starring Elizabeth Olsen, and in J.J. Abrams' new crime-drama series *Duster* (HBO Max), adding to her slate of high-profile projects.

GiGi's acting training includes the Meisner technique at Playhouse West under Robert Carnegie and comedy at The Second City Los Angeles. She has performed improv alongside Martin Short, Fred Willard, and Catherine O'Hara. Her broadcasting career encompasses news anchoring, reporting, hosting, and FM radio in both English and Spanish.

Currently, GiGi is expanding her roles as an actress, writer, and director, with plans to develop an original series, leveraging her extensive experience across multiple genres of performance and production.

About Mike Kimmel

Mike Kimmel is a former professional wrestler and circus magician. Nowadays, he is a film, television, stage, and commercial actor and acting coach. He is a thirty-plus year member of SAG-AFTRA with extensive experience in both the New York and Los Angeles markets. He has worked with directors Francis Ford Coppola, Robert Townsend, Craig Shapiro, and Christopher Cain among many others. TV credits include *Game of Silence*, *Zoo*, *Treme*, *In Plain Sight*, *Cold Case*, *Breakout Kings*, *Memphis Beat*, *Suit Up*, *Buffy The Vampire Slayer*, and *The Oprah Winfrey Show*. He was a regular sketch comedy player on *The Tonight Show*, performing live on stage and in pretaped segments with Jay Leno for eleven years. He also performed regularly with Gilbert Gottfried on USA Channel's comedic series *Up All Night*.

Mike has appeared in dozens of theatrical plays on both coasts, including Radio City Music Hall, Equity Library Theater, Stella Adler Theater, Double Image Theater, The Village Gate, and Theater at the Improv. He trained with Michael Shurtleff, William Hickey, Ralph Marrero, Gloria Maddox, Harold Sylvester, Wendy Davis, Amy Hunter, Bob Collier, and Stuart Robinson. He holds a B.A. from Brandeis University and an M.A. from California State University at Dominguez Hills.

He has taught at Upper Iowa University, University of New Orleans, University of Phoenix, Glendale Community College, Nunez Community College, Delgado Community College, and in the Los Angeles, Beverly Hills, and Burbank, California public school districts. He is a two-time past president of New Orleans Toastmasters, the public speaking organization.

Mike has written and collaborated on numerous scripts for stage and screen. *In Lincoln's Footsteps*, his full-length historical drama on Presidents Lincoln and Garfield, was a semi-finalist in the National Playwrights Conference at the Eugene O'Neill Theater Center. Mike also received the Excellence in Teaching Award from Upper Iowa University and was a founding member of the Flambeaux Theater Company in New Orleans.

In 2019, the Independent Author Network selected his third book, *Monologues for Teens*, as their Performing Arts Book of the Year. In 2022, Best Indie Book Award (BIBA) honored *Monologues for Adults* as their annual winner in the performing arts category. Mike is also prominently featured in Francis Ford Coppola's groundbreaking book on his innovative theater-film hybrid process, *Live Cinema*.

Mike is a full voting member of the National Academy of Television Arts and Sciences, the organization that produces the Emmy Awards each year. This is his twelfth book in the performing arts.

A Bold and Humble Request

If you've enjoyed *50 Secrets Nobody Tells You in Hollywood*—and feel that it would benefit our fellow actors and teachers—then please consider leaving a brief book review on the merchant site where you purchased it.

Book reviews are incredibly helpful for both authors and readers, particularly in a highly specific genre like the performing arts. Reviews help spread the word to readers looking for new material, and also help authors reach a wider audience.

Book Reviews

https://amazon.com/review/create-review?&asin=B0FQ8SN9J5

Additionally, we hope you'll consider recommending this book to your local public library or university library. Schools and libraries can often purchase books at a significant discount. In this way, the book can be made available to readers who may not be able to purchase copies for themselves.

"The worst thing one can do is not to try, to be aware of what one wants and not give in to it, to spend years in silent hurt wondering if something could have materialized—never knowing."

Jim Rohn

www.ingramcontent.com/pod-product-compliance
Lightning Source LLC
Chambersburg PA
CBHW070053080526
44586CB00013B/1038